CAF HOW TO

Fundra[...]
for
Education

A step by step guide

KAREN GILCHRIST

CAF

Published by Charities Aid Foundation
Kings Hill
West Malling
Kent ME19 4TA

Series Editor Graham Watson

Editor Myra Bennett

Design and typesetting GreenGate Publishing Services

Cover design Eugenie Dodd Typographics

Cover illustration Emma Dodd

Printed and bound in Great Britain by Bell & Bain Limited, Glasgow

A catalogue record for this book is available from the British Library

ISBN 1-85934-083-0

Telephone +44 (0) 1732 520000
Fax +44 (0) 1732 520001
E-mail Cafpubs@caf.charitynet.org

Website http://www.charitynet.org

Contents

About the author

Karen Gilchrist is a researcher and writer. She is the director of the media and communications company Resource Base which works in social, educational and cultural affairs. Karen was a journalist with the magazines *Marketing Week* and *Televisual* before working in television as a social action researcher. She has been a cross-media co-ordinator with the charity Community Service Volunteers and worked for TVS Education and Community before helping to set up Resource Base. The company runs media and communications training courses for charities and produces a wide range of resources in all media.

Introduction

Fundraising for education used to be fairly small scale and quite controversial. Now it is growing in importance.

Voluntary funding can enrich education, creating new opportunities, partnerships and projects for children in their early years or at school-age. And with the creation of partnerships such as Education Action Zones we are seeing schools, community groups, businesses, government and others working together in new ways.

It could be argued, though, that enriching one child's education disadvantages another who doesn't have access to such opportunities. It is also increasingly difficult to make the distinction between what is essential and what is enrichment. And if you don't have a resource you feel you need, you're probably more worried about getting the money to buy it than defining whether or not it is an 'essential' or an 'enrichment'.

Many funders, though, try to draw such distinctions. And parents and staff can feel uncomfortable with fundraising for certain things. You need to be aware of these sensitivities and act accordingly.

Who is the guide for?

This guide is for anyone who is fundraising on behalf of an educational organisation such as a school, pre-school or charity closely connected with one or more learning institutions. It is not intended for those involved in large-scale higher or further education fundraising, although people involved in such work might find a few useful pointers in the guide.

On a personal level, you might be a member of teaching staff working in a voluntary capacity, you might be a governor or parent, you might be a local fundraiser or 'friend' of the organisation.

If you already have some fundraising experience you might want to dip into relevant sections for tips and details of useful organisations. On the other hand, if you are relatively new to fundraising then this guide will help you get started – we suggest various processes that might be worth considering and techniques that can improve your chances of success.

Why is the guide needed?

FUNDRAISING IS A COMPETITIVE BUSINESS

Your ideas, projects and applications will almost always be weighed against another organisation's equally deserving cause. This guide is designed to help you present the positive elements of your proposal effectively, to give your application an edge, or to make your personal plea more persuasive.

YOUR TIME IS PROBABLY LIMITED

Fundraising for education is often a task taken on by busy people juggling other priorities. This guide aims to give a clear explanation of some of the funding opportunities and to signpost helpful organisations.

YOU CAN LEARN FROM OTHER PEOPLE'S SUCCESSES AND FAILURES

Other people can inspire and reinvigorate your efforts. It's not always easy to find out how other people have approached school fundraising. This guide incorporates case studies and helpful suggestions from people who have had a degree of fundraising success.

SCHEMES AND THEMES CHANGE

New funding bodies, networks and priorities come on stream and it can be hard to keep track. This guide highlights some of the emerging opportunities and suggests ways of staying in touch.

The cultural challenge

ADDING EXTRA

'Why do you need to raise funds? Surely the government should invest in the cost of a child's education.'

This is still a fairly common response when someone is asked to contribute some money to an educational cause. However, many people now appreciate that educational institutions have a wider role to play in the community. Some organisations need additional facilities to support pupils who are disadvantaged by local circumstances or their family environment. And there is plenty of scope to create educational opportunities that are not at the core of the curriculum.

Trusts and companies are nervous of stepping in where government has pulled out. They often have clauses excluding the funding of anything which is, or used to be, covered by statutory sources. Parents and governors are also rightly concerned about paying for essentials that should be funded by the state. Importantly, they don't want to put pressure on other parents to make 'contributions' towards the cost of their child's education.

HOW VOLUNTARY IS 'VOLUNTARY'?

The DfEE is clear in its guidance to governors (*School Governors: A Guide to The Law*): 'all requests to parents for voluntary contributions must make it clear that the contributions would be voluntary. You should also make it clear that children of parents who do not contribute will not be treated differently.' This advice is given in the context of charging for activities in school time. However, it is just as relevant when extended to educational fundraising in general.

YOUR POSITION

Parents and potential funders often feel more comfortable if you have a clear statement about the scope of your fundraising. You might first want to identify those aspects of your work which you consider absolutely ring-fenced and core-funded. And then you can turn to those elements which would make a difference to students and the local community, in line with wider educational and social objectives.

We return to this issue at various points throughout the guide. For the moment, though, it's important to note that attitudes towards external funding are changing, the funding environment is also changing, and the distinctions between essentials and extras, statutory and non-statutory, voluntary and partnership are blurring.

A brief overview

- Chapter 1 looks at an essential fundraising reference – the organisation's development plan. Fundraising doesn't take place in a vacuum. It must fit in with the overall goals of the organisation. We stress the need to avoid *ad hoc* fundraising bursts. And we discuss the importance of building coherent plans.
- Chapter 2 talks you through a mapping activity to help you identify some of the sources of funding and assistance available. It is important to identify these from the outset. Some people and organisations can help with your fundraising efforts. Others might be obvious sources of funds. Once you have a clear idea of who can help, you can start to prioritise your fundraising efforts. And you can approach the appropriate people with different proposals. This mapping is one of the elements you will include in your fundraising strategy.
- Chapter 3 looks in more detail at producing a fundraising strategy. We describe the essential ingredients and the importance of developing a strategy to suit your circumstances. The strategy is a living document and should be revised over time.
- Chapter 4 focuses on project planning. Sometimes it will be easy to identify a project – a cultural exchange, an

environmental initiative, an artist's residency, etc as a project – all have obvious beginnings and endings, and measurable aims. It might be more difficult to see a piece of computer equipment, some library books or the re-surfacing of a car park as projects. However, it is important to frame your various fundraising initiatives in this way. This will help you to identify the need for the funding, the work involved and the potential outcomes. It will help with your own planning and assist funders to assess your request for support.

We move on to some of the main sources of funding in the next three chapters. We look at how to get up to date information about available funding. And we discuss some of the ways to improve your chances of success.

- Chapter 5 looks at local, central and European Government funding.
- Chapter 6 explores funding from trusts, foundations and the National Lottery.
- Businesses at a local and national level contribute to the education sector in various ways and we look at some of the opportunities in Chapter 7.
- Community fundraising – raising money at a local level from individuals – is used quite frequently by schools and small community organisations. However, it often takes a lot of effort for fairly low levels of income. In Chapter 8, we look at some of the ways you can raise money in your neighbourhood and suggest ways of making your community fundraising more effective.
- Databases are a useful fundraising tool and we devote Chapter 9 to this issue. We stress the importance of keeping track of your fundraising efforts, and the need to keep people informed.
- In Building on Success, Chapter 10, we look at the need for evaluation, publicity and feedback as you develop ongoing relationships with your funders.
- Finally, we list useful sources of information and advice.

CHAPTER 1

Development planning

This chapter focuses on the need for identity and direction in your fundraising efforts; people need to be clear about what you are trying to achieve and why voluntary funds are needed. Everyone involved needs to understand how voluntary fundraising can make a difference and the majority of people connected with your organisation need to think it is appropriate and worthwhile.

Putting fundraising into context

Some people occasionally set up small fundraising events for specific items. Or they get involved in a major appeal for a single project. But increasingly educational fundraising is ongoing. Fundraising needs to be set in a broader context.

You need to know why you are raising money. And if you are fundraising as a separate associated organisation, you need to be clear that the relevant governing or management body:

- wants (and needs) your money;
- will accept your donation;
- will spend it as you (and any other donors) intend it to be spent.

If you are fundraising for another organisation, for instance as 'friends' of a school, then their business or development plan is an essential reference. This will give you guidance on their funded core activities, the overall direction they are going in and the opportunities for extra funding to make a difference.

At the same time you will need to consult their fundraising policy, to find out what is and is not acceptable in terms of fundraising methods, gifts in kind, and approaches to parents, staff and people who have links with the organisation (in the case of schools, this might mean past pupils).

Who is doing the fundraising?

THE FUNDRAISING ORGANISATION

There might seem to be an obvious answer to the question 'who is doing the fundraising?' But it is still worth asking because there might be more than one person or group seeking money on behalf of an organisation.

Combining and co-ordinating your efforts will prevent the potential embarrassment of competing appeals and will mean you can achieve more together than you could individually.

YOUR PERSONAL ROLE IN FUNDRAISING ACTIVITIES

You also need to ask 'in what capacity am I fundraising?'

This is particularly important if you are an employee of a community, foundation or aided school. If your wages are being paid for by the state then you are expected to spend your working time on core school activities. Fundraising efforts for additional items should really be done in your own time as a volunteer.

The other issue raised by this question is the status of any fundraising body you are working for.

WHAT IS YOUR CONSTITUTION?

If you are a charitable organisation offering early years education or out of school activities, then you will probably be clear about your status. You might be a volunteer or employee of that charity. If, however, you are part of a friends organisation linked with a school then things can be a bit more complicated. And this needs a little discussion.

SCHOOL FUNDRAISING BODIES

There are many different types of school and educational institutions, all with unique histories and local circumstances. Schools themselves have a variety of management structures. Governing bodies, or boards of management, have different powers and responsibilities, depending on the type of school concerned. And a number of institutions are going through their own process of evolution. All of this means that there is no single appropriate model for a school fundraising body.

But there are some principles to bear in mind and some options to consider. We outline these below, but recommend you consult widely before reaching any structural decisions. Your local education authority may be able to advise you. If you are an aided school, then your founding body (eg your diocesan board) could give you guidance.

Teaching unions, the National Council for Parent–Teacher Associations, and the Charity Commission are among others who might provide helpful advice (see Further information, page 127).

PRINCIPLES TO CONSIDER

You should bear the following principles in mind:

- A school governing body doesn't have to raise additional money or accept donations.
- If your organisation holds voluntary funds for the 'advancement of education' then you might have set up a charitable trust.
- Most charities in England and Wales with an income of more than £1,000 need to register with the Charity Commission (there are some exceptions).
- Governors should clearly identify any money that comes into a school budget as voluntary funding, rather than from statutory sources or founding bodies.
- Fundraising bodies need to be clear about the scope of their work, and be open to scrutiny.

- School fundraising bodies need to complement and enhance the work of the school, consult and reflect the views of parents, governors and other interested parties.
- Beneficiaries (who gain from voluntary fundraising) should not be trustees (who hold the money raised).

STRUCTURES TO CONSIDER

At its simplest you could:

- Re-activate an existing, but dormant, relevant fundraising body.
- Fundraise as an individual voluntary 'agent' for the governing or managing body and donate funds directly to the organisation's budget.

Or you could consider the following options (not all are mutually exclusive).

Setting up a trust fund

Setting up a trust fund under direct management of the governing body or management committee might be an appropriate structure for some schools. It means that the 'owners' of the school budget manage additional external funding directly, making planning easier. A 'trust' holds money or assets on trust for other people or organisations. It does not own property or money in its own right. Before setting up this kind of structure you should consult your LEA to see if they are happy with this arrangement and can advise you on how to go about it. You might also want to involve your own solicitors for independent advice.

Setting up a trust under joint trusteeship

Setting up a trust under joint trusteeship of the governing body and a home-school association (or friends organisation) could create a greater sense of partnership. Again, it is worth consulting your LEA to see what is acceptable and appropriate, before asking an independent solicitor for advice.

Establishing a community education trust

You could set up a community education trust for a number of schools, colleges, pre-schools, etc across a borough, district, city or county. This enables you to fundraise on a larger scale, showing benefits across a wider area to potential funders. This in turn can make your funding proposals more attractive – their money can have a more extensive impact. If you are considering setting up a community education trust, then it is worth consulting your LEA to see if they have any plans or can assist you in doing this.

Setting up a separate associated charity

Fundraising is not in itself a charitable object. Fundraising must be carried out to support the charitable purposes of the organisation (the relief of poverty and sickness; the advancement of education for public benefit; the advancement of religion for public benefit; or other legally defined 'purposes beneficial to the community').

Charitable status means that you can approach a number of grant making trusts which only donate money to charities. It brings a number of tax reliefs. And it can change people's attitudes to your organisation. Some companies, for instance, only spend their community affairs budgets on charities (sometimes only registered charities). To find out more about setting up a charity contact the Charity Commission (see Further information, page 121). They can advise you on whether or not you need to register with them and the legal documents and processes required.

Most charities with an income of £1,000 or more each year must register. There are specific rules on different types of schools; grant maintained schools, for example, are exempt from this requirement. Once your income exceeds £10,000 per year you must submit a narrative report with your accounts.

Incorporating an association

You could incorporate an association to secure limited liability for any debts incurred in good faith. A corporate body (or incorporated association) has a separate legal identity from the individual members, directors or trustees. If those individuals act in good faith, on appropriate advice and with due prudence then, in most cases, their liability is limited to the assets of the corporate body. All governing bodies are incorporated.

If a group is unincorporated it has no separate legal identity – all members are equally liable for debts the group incurs (including past members). An unincorporated organisation cannot enter into contracts or hold assets; individual members must do so on behalf of the group. If you want to fundraise as a group and hand money over to another body to administer, then it might be appropriate to remain as an unincorporated group. You can also become an independent trust or association, whilst remaining unincorporated. You should discuss your status with members of your group and an independent solicitor.

Creating a separate company for trading

Making a distinction between your main organisation and a separate trading company helps ensure than no cross-subsidising occurs. The key benefits of creating a company are:

- a trading company offers a distinct body quite separate from your main organisation;
- if the trading company incurs any liabilities or debts this does not mean that your main organisation is affected;
- the trading company provides you with limited personal liability;
- the trading company has a clear financial and legal identity and can enter into contracts with other organisations and individuals.

It is worth consulting a solicitor and accountant for help in setting up a trading company. This will ensure that you set up the appropriate structures. If you are a charity then you might want to get advice from the Charity Commission on what is acceptable and appropriate.

CASE STUDY

A small primary school was struggling to attract pupils and felt that some form of pre-school provision would help to boost its reception class numbers. After consulting locally, the governors discovered a number of local businesses needed nursery facilities for their staff. A separate charity was established and trust funding was secured for the cost of building facilities. Ongoing revenue was provided by local businesses through fees and sponsorship. Parents within the wider community also had low-cost access to childcare. And the number of children in the school's reception class doubled.

Formal structures might seem to involve a lot of effort if your fundraising is still in its infancy, but they can help establish clear boundaries and relationships which become more important as you start to build up donations.

The development plan

We have already said that the organisation's development plan is a vital starting point for any fundraising. The plan contains some very practical information about how the organisation hopes to grow over the next few years. And you will start to see some of the areas where voluntary income could make a major difference.

The development plan should highlight medium to long-term goals which set a direction and tone to be adopted in your fundraising efforts.

The development plan will grow and change over time. It should capture the spirit of the organisation, reflecting the aims and aspirations of everyone involved.

DEMONSTRATING A COHERENT APPROACH

Working from the development plan will ensure that everyone is working to similar objectives. And it also means you can demonstrate to a potential funder that your proposals fit into a clear and coherent plan.

EMERGING PROJECTS

The development plan will have highlighted a number of areas in need of voluntary funding.

In some cases several needs could be brought together into a single project. For instance, the resurfacing of a car park could be combined with the need for an environmental study area and developed into a 'green improvement' or landscaping project. Other elements will be distinct.

Your list of areas in need of voluntary funding might include:

- **whole-organisation initiatives**: charters, policies, themed cross-curricular events, such as Science Week or Europe Day;
- **the physical environment**: access, playground, conservation, landscaping, security, refurbishment, building;
- **outside hours clubs**: subject-based, after-school, sports, arts;
- **children's personal, social and emotional development**: mentoring, peer counselling;
- **resources/facilities**: equipment, materials, visiting extra-curricular teaching staff;
- **trips and exchanges:** overseas, field trips, visits;
- **residencies and performances**: workshops, plays;
- **community access and education**: sports, arts and clubs;
- **links**: joint projects with educational bodies and community groups, industry partnerships.

The list probably won't include all of the above, but it could still appear lengthy and daunting. This is why there is a need for a fundraising strategy. You need to prioritise your needs and work out what is feasible.

It is better to focus initially on a small number of fundraising priorities and to succeed than to go for an enormous wide-ranging appeal and fail.

The development plan might not be the only source of ideas for improvements needing voluntary funding. So it is worth consulting on a wider basis before coming up with a definitive list.

CASE STUDY

A High School set up a School Council of students. The Council identified a range of environmental initiatives which could benefit all students. These included tree planting, seating for outdoor areas and improvements to the bike sheds. Their ideas complemented the school development plan, but also identified additional areas for improvement. The School Council then set up a series of inter-form competitions to get the fundraising off the ground.

Identifying your resource needs

Before seeking outside funding for projects you need to look first at:

- whether savings can be made in one area to contribute towards another (considering whether or not this is allowed and possible);
- any aspects of the project which are, or should be, funded from existing budgets (so that you don't commit the error of 'double funding' – receiving funding from two sources for the same thing).

Then you can start working out how much additional money is needed to get the project started.

CHAPTER 2

Identifying potential fundraisers and supporters

Once you have worked through your development plan, and consulted with relevant people, you will start to have an idea of the scale of fundraising needed. You might be feeling that the whole task seems overwhelming and over-ambitious.

An audit of the potential goodwill and available support will hopefully give you more confidence. It will also help you to devise an appropriate fundraising strategy (see Chapter 3).

The need to audit

An audit involves:

- looking at what is already there;
- making a note or 'map' of it.

It's as simple as that. You are making an exhaustive list of the people and organisations that might offer some sort of contribution towards your fundraising.

CASE STUDY

A small rural school had four classrooms and was advised by school inspectors that it needed another two. The school had planning permission and sufficient space, but needed voluntary funding for the buildings and fittings. The governors began to consider how they could fundraise and conducted some initial research.

They found no appropriate local businesses to approach. But through their mapping of people and organisations who might make a contribution, they discovered an old dormant family trust, with an educational purpose, linked to a local museum. The school worked with the museum to reactivate the trust and set up a fundraising appeal targeting wealthy individuals in the local neighbourhood.

Mapping networks

You might start off with a simple diagram, using rings to represent an ever-widening area around your organisation.

Within these rings you can list headings for the individuals or bodies that could be of assistance in a variety of ways – as advocates, fundraising 'agents', or funders.

Your diagram would start off with a ring devoted to the organisation itself, and might look like Figure 1.

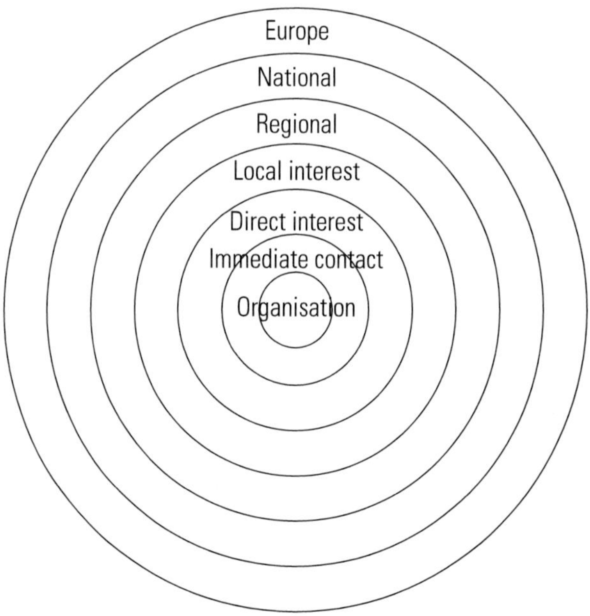

Figure 1

ORGANISATION

Within the 'organisation' circle you might highlight:

- staff (teaching and non-teaching);
- parent-teacher association/home-school association;
- volunteers;
- pupils.

It is important to remember, though, that there are strict rules on what a person under the age of 16 can do in terms of fundraising. They can be involved in a performance or display for which you sell tickets. They can carry out a sponsored activity. But they can't sell or collect door-to-door from people they don't know.

Your close colleagues, and anyone else who strongly believes in your work, are your best advocates. And good advocates make good fundraisers.

You should note that any teaching staff or other school/college employees who become involved in fundraising must do so as volunteers, in their own time, if the institution is state-funded.

CASE STUDY

A teacher at a large secondary school raised £5,000 in her own time for a peer-counselling project (students on a GNVQ community care course provide advice and support to other young people).

The teacher wrote a project plan with a group of sixth form students and successfully applied for a grant from a mental health charity. The project funding was only available to 'informal groups'.

IMMEDIATE CONTACT

'Immediate contact' might include:

- parents;
- governors;
- management committees;
- board members;
- the local education authority, etc.

This ring not only contains a number of potential fundraisers and donors, it also holds those who should be treated with the greatest sensitivity when you are fundraising. No-one should feel pressured to be involved in your voluntary fundraising activities. And no-one should be put in an uncomfortable position if they are unable to contribute. Remember that you are not begging for money. You are asking people to contribute to something that they believe in and care about.

DIRECT INTEREST

People and organisations with a 'direct interest' in your organisation might include:

- former staff and pupils;
- associated organisations, for instance, feeder schools.

Former staff and pupils might want to leave a sum of money to their old school in their will. They will certainly want to know how the organisation is developing. They might be interested in coming to reunions. A good way to stay in touch is to send them a regular newsletter, and to invite them to update you on what they are currently doing.

You can benefit from tracking their progress. If an ex-pupil achieves something newsworthy then that is worth mentioning in your publicity material. A famous ex-student might make a good patron for the fundraising group (and they might attend the occasional event too, attracting larger audiences). An ex-pupil in a position of authority within a company might be able to make a sizeable donation to your fund.

CASE STUDY

A young pop group with a large local following put on a benefit concert for their old school and donated all of the profits – £3,000 – to the school minibus fund.

Not every ex-pupil will end up as a rich, powerful or famous person. However, many people will retain a long-term interest in their old school and in the progress of their old friends in later life. And for a number this interest might extend to leaving a small legacy to your organisation. Further information on legacies is contained in a book published jointly by the Charities Aid Foundation and Institute of Charity Fundraising Managers (see Further information, page 127).

It is also important for you to operate within the Data Protection Act when contacting former pupils and staff, and we discuss this in more detail in Chapter 9, page 111.

Joint initiatives with other educational organisations (such as feeder or receiving schools) can help with fundraising efforts – making the numbers involved more attractive for funders.

CASE STUDY

Three feeder primary schools and their secondary school secured project funding from an environmental charity and a local business to develop a joint schools' nature area. Pupils worked as volunteers on some of the practical conservation work. The schools continue to work together on the nature area. The link with the local business has continued, and the firm has funded the development of new resource materials and offered work experience opportunities to secondary school students.

CASE STUDY

A secondary school formed a 'family of schools' with feeder primaries to raise money to improve the community environment. Funding for the initiative came from the police authority, a local tenants association and the rotary club.

LOCAL INTEREST

The 'local interest' section of your chart could include:

- community education trusts (if there are any in your area);
- support agencies (such as education-business partnerships);
- small family trusts;
- Rotary clubs;
- tenants' associations;
- local authority departments;
- local celebrity/philanthropists;
- parish and town councils;
- local businesses.

These potential donors might have relatively small funding budgets, but you will only be competing with a small number of other schools and community groups when you approach them.

CASE STUDY

A large primary school received financial support from its education-business partnership (EBP) to develop and print a series of family-based learning materials. The EBP secured additional support from the Training and Enterprise Council (TEC) towards the production of the three books, which encourage parents and siblings to help children with their reading and study skills. (For more information on EBPs and TECs, see Chapter 5, page 60.)

Local support agencies and partnerships will be familiar with your local community. And they might well have attended some of your events or seen them mentioned in the paper. Given all of these factors, your success rate is likely to be higher than when you target people nationally. The amount of money you raise per donation, though, might be less!

REGIONAL

At a regional level there are a variety of organisations which might offer support. These include:

- medium-sized companies;
- media groups;
- trusts covering one or two counties:
- the police and health authorities:
- various quasi autonomous non-governmental organisations (quangos) such as the regional development agency and regional arts board (see Chapter 5, page 59).

CASE STUDY

A parent-staff association raised over £2,000 from an ITV company's community affairs budget for playground equipment. A member of the parent-staff association attended a media training event at which the ITV company promoted its community giving. Building on this initial contact the group submitted a request for funding which was considered and approved at the company's quarterly community donations meeing.

NATIONAL

Under the 'national' heading you will highlight various government schemes or departments. In some cases you might be thinking of quangos. At others you will be considering national initiatives which are implemented at regional or local level.

You might also be able to approach national trusts and foundations with a particular interest in your geographical area or the group of people you are targeting. Companies at a national level might also have particular funding schemes that are appropriate. We will look at all of these areas in greater detail in subsequent chapters. But it is worth noting any national companies which employ parents of pupils attending the school. Some run what's known as 'match-funding' initiatives. This means that the company donates a sum of money equal to that raised or donated by their employee. In effect it doubles the gift.

CASE STUDY

A pre-school playgroup raised £500 when a trustee ran a mini-marathon. But at the same time it hit its fundraising target of £1,000 to buy a range of new musical instruments. The trustee worked for a company which offered match-funding to staff involved in 'good causes'. The firm matched her sponsorship pound for pound.

EUROPE

When you reach the 'Europe' ring you might think this is a waste of time – too much bureaucracy, too complicated, bewildering, or just too big for what you want to do. But there are European initiatives that might be applicable, and there are centres based in the UK which can help you find out what's available. There is also a Website highlighting funding opportunities (see page 128). Don't dismiss European help as being inappropriate. It's worth considering, even if only to obtain some relevant free resource materials.

It might be appropriate to link up with a number of partners to bid for European funding.

CASE STUDY

A local authority community education department set up an umbrella bid for European funding. Ten organisations had done some initial fundraising for their local projects. This funding could be doubled, if they applied for match funding from Europe. However, the groups concerned did not have the time or expertise to bid for European funding on their own or to find transnational partners. The local authority completed the forms and made a successful bid.

Recording information

Once you have developed your broad headings you can start to be more specific: identifying a particular local business as a potential supporter, or a national foundation or trust as worth approaching. You can start to build up a database of current and potential donors, ensuring that you remain within the rules of the Data Protection Act (see page 111).

It is very important to record any contact you have with potential funders. This will allow you to track your progress, to build relationships with the various people concerned, and to ensure that, should you have to give up your fundraising role, someone could pick up where you have left off.

Now that you have a clear idea of the potential support available you can start work on your fundraising strategy.

CHAPTER 3

Designing a fundraising strategy

A fundraising strategy is a plan of practical and achievable steps. It outlines how you move from your current position to where you want to be within a timeframe of, for instance, five years. It also describes the mix of funding you hope to achieve – from government, trusts, companies and the community.

Your development plan already provides an essential framework, highlighting broad goals and key areas of interest. The mapping exercise, or audit of friends and supporters, will have given you an overview of who you can approach for help.

Now you can put these things together and develop:

- a list of priorities;
- an action plan;
- a timetable.

The main ingredients

In this section we are going to focus on the elements that you might want to include in your fundraising strategy.

AN INTRODUCTION

The strategy is a living document – in other words it will change and develop over time. Because of this it is likely to be referred to by a variety of people in different circumstances. You can't guarantee that they will have read any background documents, such as your development plan or your audit of supporters.

It is therefore important to begin your fundraising strategy with an 'introduction' which talks about supporting research documents and quotes relevant information. You might want to attach these other papers in full or in part as appendices.

An assessment of your position

Your audit of supporters will have shown you some of the potential help at hand. Whilst these supporters are on the map they remain 'potential'. Can you convert them into active supporters?

You need to look at your particular circumstances and ask questions like: 'who are we competing with for funds?' and 'are local families in any position to provide extra financial support?'.

A SWOT analysis is a useful tool to help you carry out an assessment of your position.

SWOT ANALYSIS

SWOT stands for Strengths, Weaknesses, Opportunities, and Threats. This analysis technique is used by businesses, local government and the voluntary sector to give a realistic picture of a particular organisation, product or service.

When you do a SWOT analysis, the aim is both to look inwards at your organisation and outwards to compare it with other organisations who are competing for funds. SWOT analysis should help you spot the qualities that make your cause unique and deserving. And it should also give you an idea of your relative chances of success with different funders.

Your SWOT analysis will enable you to build on your strengths; compensate for any weaknesses; make the most of the opportunities; and take action against any threats.

SWOT analyses are best done as a brainstorm by a number of people. You need to be constructive and honest. Do not allow it to become a platform for people to moan.

You need the analysis to be totally relevant for your fundraising strategy. For instance, you might say that a strength of your organisation is that 'the staff are very committed to the college.' This is obviously a 'good thing', but how is it relevant to fundraising? It would be better to say: 'the staff are very committed to the college and are prepared to spend some of their spare time on fundraising activities' or 'the staff are very committed to the college, a commitment which would impress potential funders', etc.

You might include the following in your SWOT analysis:

- The local economy and the social background of young people and their families (some things that appear as weaknesses in one way could also be fundraising strengths – for instance: a high proportion of disadvantaged families might mean few appropriate opportunities for local fundraising events, but at the same time it might mean that a national charitable trust would offer support because 'education of disadvantaged families' is a funding priority).
- Your fundraising body and its relationship with the associated school, college, etc.
- The object of your fundraising, ie the school, college, pre-school, etc, as an institution.
- Relationships with existing funders, potential funders, and others.

In each case you work through the four aspects of the table in Figure 2 below.

Strengths	Weaknesses
Opportunities	Threats

Figure 2

A POSITION STATEMENT

In addition to carrying out a SWOT analysis you might want to include a general statement about your approach to fundraising (a position statement). This statement will say something about why you are fundraising and the sources of money you consider appropriate. You might rule out appeals to parents, for example, in this position statement. Or you might limit your fundraising requests which target parents to up to two sponsorship events per year.

You could include a reference to donations of equipment, such as computers or vehicles, saying what would and would not be considered appropriate.

Employing a professional fundraiser

At this stage you could consider whether or not you want to employ a professional fundraiser.

A professional fundraiser is defined as someone who raises money on your behalf and is paid £5 or more a day or £500 or more in a year for this work. If you pay a consultant for general advice on your fundraising strategy this would not be considered 'professional fundraising'.

The Charities Act lays down strict rules for the employment of professional fundraisers, and you should read through these before taking someone on.

The rules mean that:

- you must have a written agreement in place before a professional fundraiser makes an appeal for money or property on your behalf;
- a professional fundraiser can only claim the remuneration and expenses that are outlined in the written agreement;
- every time a professional fundraiser approaches a donor they need to state: the name of the organisation concerned; how they will be remunerated themselves; how any sums of money

will be divided between different organisations; what proportion of money from the sale of a product will go to the organisation, etc;
- the fundraiser mustn't claim you are a charity if you are not.

Professional fundraisers have a wealth of knowledge, skills and contacts. These, of course, come at a price. You need to weigh up the costs and benefits and decide if you want to make such an investment for the medium and long-term returns. A scrupulous fundraiser will not take on the work if they think it isn't the right approach or that the returns for you would be too low. If you want more information then contact the Institute of Charity Fundraising Managers (ICFM).

Building a strategy that works for you

Now you need to ensure the strategy meets your particular needs by drawing up a list of fundraising priorities.

SETTING PRIORITIES

Your priorities could begin as a simple list of all the things you want to raise money for – taken from your organisation's development plan. However, the list will remain a wishlist until you grade things by their importance and turn them into priorities.

If you are fundraising for an associated organisation, it is essential to work with this organisation when you set your priorities. For instance, a head teacher might have said 'wouldn't it be nice to have a swimming pool' as a throwaway remark. Really they might be more concerned to host a support course for exceptionally gifted children, or to set up literacy groups for parents from minority ethnic communities. It would be inappropriate for an associated fundraising body to focus all its efforts and energies on raising money for the swimming pool under such circumstances.

If a number of your priorities appear to be smaller parts of a whole you might find it easier to raise money for them as a single project.

In listing your priorities ask yourself:

- Why is this a priority?
- How will the community, young people in particular, benefit?

This will help you to start thinking in terms that will appeal to potential funders.

MAKING AN ACTION PLAN

Once you have come up with your list of priorities you can start building a realistic action plan and timetable to achieve them.

A fundraising action plan is not the same as an individual project plan (which is discussed in Chapter 4). The fundraising action plan talks in broad terms about several funding priorities or projects. It doesn't contain a breakdown of how project money will be spent or detailed information about the resulting benefits.

A fundraising action plan:

- has one or more funding targets (with supporting budgets);
- identifies potential (relevant) sources of funding;
- outlines the steps needed to raise the necessary money.

These steps might include general marketing initiatives, such as sending out promotional postcards, as well as more specific activities, such as sending out funding proposals.

It can be helpful to ask some general questions such as:

- Who might want to put additional funding into our organisation/projects?
- Why would anyone give us any money?

You might feel that certain projects stand a good chance of getting funding from a charitable trust. Some projects might clearly fit in with a government initiative. Others might need funding from a mixture of sources.

CASE STUDY

When a school began fundraising for a new community arts building the fundraisers adopted an approach used by many hospice appeals. They set up a number of advisory committees drawn from influential people who 'pyramid fundraised' from friends, associates and connected organisations. After a year of this approach they then (as planned) launched a public appeal.

What might be included, then, in your action plan?

- time to prepare project plans (which are discussed in more detail in the following chapter);
- a research phase into potential funders;
- details of how you intend to approach potential funders;
- fundraising events (if appropriate);
- a review of your funding position and budget;
- further approaches (if necessary);
- evaluation of fundraising;
- project implementation;
- development of relationship with funders.

General activities to plot on your fundraising action plan, include:

- promotional events and materials (including brochures and newsletters);
- database development;
- networking or attendance at meetings of relevant umbrella organisations/support agencies;
- activities to foster the development of donor relationships;
- consultation meetings;
- regular fundraising events (eg Christmas Fair, Valentine's Ball);
- reporting and accounting.

PUTTING TOGETHER A TIMETABLE

You need to put together a timetable for your various actions to give a clear idea of what is needed and by when.

The timetable is often presented in a flow chart or 'Gant chart', showing the various stages as blocks of time. This doesn't mean that each stage takes a month to complete, merely that it should happen within this month. The chart can be plotted against a calendar and if anything happens to cause a delay, everything can simply be moved on to a later date (see Figure 3 and Figure 4).

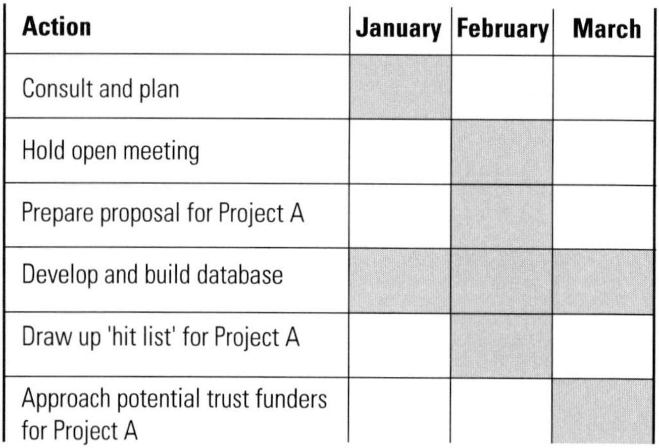

Figure 3 Extract from action plan Gant chart

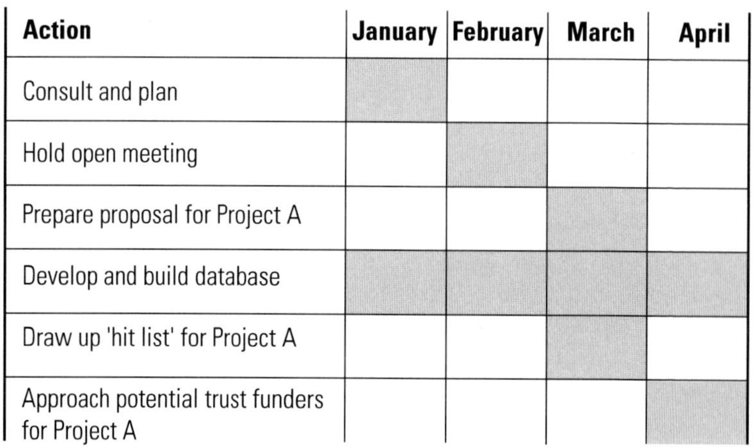

Figure 4 Extract from a revised action plan Gant chart

You can see from Figure 3 that if the proposal for Project A could not be prepared on time, then the remainder of the action plan could easily be pushed on.

If you want to develop several projects at once, then your chart will be much more detailed with a number of shaded areas running in parallel. Support work common to all projects (such as database development) should also be shown.

Defining roles

Your action planning will give you a fair idea of the amount of time and effort required. Educational fundraising is frequently done in people's own volunteered time. It is rarely done by one person alone (although at times it can feel like that for the committed fundraiser).

The fundraising strategy provides an opportunity to define some of the roles and associated tasks for your fundraising team. If you name roles rather than individuals this means that the plan is still valid when circumstances change and people move on. If you define a role this allows people to decide whether or not they want to commit themselves to what is involved. It will also help you to judge whether or not someone has the relevant skills or needs additional support and training.

Some of the fundraising roles you might define include:

- administrator;
- trust fundraiser;
- corporate donations and sponsorship fundraiser;
- major appeals organiser;
- events co-ordinator;
- school liaison/link person;
- publicist.

An individual might fulfil several of the above roles at the same time.

You might also want to approach an appropriate person to act as a patron for your organisation as a whole or for a particular appeal.

Setting a budget

As well as putting together a general timetable for your action plan, you will need to prepare a fundraising budget. You might be happy at present for various people to beaver away as volunteers, using personal facilities. But there will come a time when your fundraising costs some money. For instance, you might want to cover expenses incurred by people attending committee or networking meetings. You might want to print some general promotional material.

Since fundraising for education is mostly done in people's own time, your overall fundraising budget is likely to be quite small (hundreds rather than thousands of pounds). But it is worth introducing a formal budget so that everyone is clear about what can be done and where the money is coming from. It might also help you to identify resources and services that can be provided in kind by people linked with your group – and to put a value on these.

As soon as you start to budget and spend money you will need someone to take responsibility for maintaining the group's accounts. We return to the issue of budgets on page 45.

In the next chapter we look at the preparation of project plans.

CHAPTER 4

Developing individual project plans

There is one further planning issue to cover before we move on to potential sources of funding, and techniques to help secure support: this is project planning.

The need for project plans

Project planning is a vital tool if you are applying to any kind of organisation for money. Businesses, trusts and government bodies all want to be confident that their money will be spent effectively. Many will request a project plan before they offer funding.

WHAT IS A PROJECT PLAN?

Your fundraising priorities become your projects. A project plan describes:

- why you want to do something;
- how much it will cost;
- how you will achieve it (once funded);
- how you will assess whether or not you have been successful.

WHY PROJECT PLANS ARE HELPFUL

Project plans are helpful because they provide:

- the basis of a fundraising proposal;
- a document which everyone can 'sign up to', ensuring all concerned are agreed about the way forward;
- a chance to consider all aspects of the work which need funding;

- an opportunity to highlight elements of the project which could be provided in kind;
- the outline of a process which can be adopted by someone else if you are unable to implement it.

CASE STUDY

A nursery school for children with special needs and their siblings applied to several trusts and foundations for a major building project. After three years sufficient money had been raised. The original fundraiser and the nursery manager had both moved on and out of the area. There was, however, a detailed project plan, including information on potential contractors. The current nursery manager was able to follow this plan, with a few amendments, to construct an entire new wing, including a much-needed sensory room.

Essential elements

So, just what should be included in a project plan?

SUMMARY OR OVERVIEW

Some people like to begin each project plan with a brief summary or overview. This can help you to focus on what you are trying to achieve. A short snappy description can be helpful if you need to fill in an application form for a potential funder. Funders often ask for an outline of your application in one or two sentences.

Such a summary can also be very helpful when you are speaking to potential funders. It gives you the basis for a quick description of your proposal. And it is also handy reference when you are looking at whether or not your project meets a funder's criteria or themes.

INTRODUCTION

An introduction sets your plan in some sort of context. You might want to include a brief reference to your organisation, its history and mission statement. You might want to talk about project partners. And you might say something about the local community, economy or other relevant background.

AIMS AND OBJECTIVES

When you are outlining the aims and objectives of your plan, it is important to relate them to people where you can.

So, rather than saying: 'our aim is to develop an arts centre on the college site'; it would be preferable to say something like: 'our aim is to develop an arts centre to offer students a diversity of cultural experiences and to attract people from the community into the college environment.' People can begin to see the project in terms of how it affects and benefits others.

Your objectives should flow from your aims. They should be measurable, so you might want to mention specific targets. Among other things, they might refer to the following:

- Community involvement– you need to say how you intend to involve the community and how widely you want to consult and involve them.
- Quality – project objectives usually mention quality. This might be in terms of particular goods or services, the experiences of participants, or the overall management of the project.
- Equal opportunities – you will want to ensure that everyone has access to your facilities and no-one is discriminated against. The project might address the needs of particular groups of people who could be disadvantaged.
- The project in a wider context – you might want to tell others about your work or create a model of good practice.

OUTCOMES

Project outcomes (sometimes described as 'outputs') are a mixture of tangible products and the less visible impact on people.

They might include products such as:

- buildings;
- equipment;
- resources.

They might include effects such as:

- skills;
- attitudes;
- relationships.

METHODOLOGY

In the methodology section you explain how you will achieve all of the aims, objectives and outcomes you have previously set out. You can either present this section as a step by step process or you can divide it up into the type of work involved (such as research; consultation; tendering, etc).

EVALUATION

Good project management involves ongoing review and adjustment. It is important to include details of how you intend to monitor and evaluate progress. External funders might have additional evaluation requirements, involving an independent assessor. They would pay for any extra evaluation themselves, but you need to budget for any evaluation you want to include.

TIMETABLE

Your timetable can be linked to a calendar or can be presented as a Gant chart with blocks of time marked out. If you decide to relate your timetable to a calendar, then it is important to allow sufficient time for fundraising. Potential funders might turn your request down if they can't meet what looks to be an unachievable deadline.

Other questions to ask when reviewing your project timetable are:

- Is there enough time to recruit or contract workers?
- Is there enough time to raise awareness and recruit participants?
- How does the timetable allow for school holidays/term times, etc?
- Does the timetable include review meetings and consultation?
- Could two or three things be done simultaneously or do they have to be done one after the other?
- What would happen if something was delayed?

BUDGET

Having done all of the above planning you should have quite an exhaustive list of items of expenditure. It is still worth some sort of double-checking to make sure everything is covered. You might invite someone unconnected with the project to read through the budget for you. You might compare it with previous budgets.

So, what might your budget include?

People

If you are using a professional, such as a solicitor or architect, then you need to include a cost for their fees. If they offer to provide their services at a discount or at no cost then you should show this within your budget. The true value should be shown as a cost and then the discount or 'in kind' donation of their time should be displayed as income.

Sadly, the 'in kind' donation doesn't apply to the time donated by volunteers to general fundraising or project management. If your organisation is employing someone to carry out this work then this can be shown as a true cost based on the time involved.

Hired facilities

Under this heading you might include room hire (eg for a one-off course or a regular event), equipment hire (eg audio visual kit), and any other items which you are using temporarily for the project.

Materials

You might need to buy a range of products. Some might be ready to use 'off-the-shelf', others might need to be adapted or specially created for your project.

Promotion

Within this heading you might include the design and production of a variety of marketing tools for the project – from posters through to Websites.

Expenses

Calculating expenses isn't easy. Expenses include the cost of travel, accommodation and food incurred by people carrying out work on the project. If you have an advisory group, for instance, you might want to pay their occasional travel expenses. Alternatively, paying for the travel expenses of parents involved in a family learning project might be a fundamental everyday part of the project.

Overheads

If your project is going to have a temporary base and staff, then the associated overheads should be itemised in your budget.

Communication support

If you are to ensure everyone has equal access to your project you might need to pay for sign language interpretation, an induction loop, a personal assistant's costs, translation, etc.

Insurance

The appropriate insurance policies will depend on the type of project you are running. If you need advice, then consult an independent financial adviser who should provide guidance and will obtain competitive quotes for you. You might need to consider public liability insurance if you are organising an event. Theft insurance might also be helpful if various people are handling cash on your group's behalf.

Contingency

It is usual to include a sum of money for unforeseen circumstances. This might even cover the cost of inflation if it takes some time to find sufficient funding for your project. The usual level of contingency is between five and ten per cent.

As well as detailing any in kind support as income against the budget heading, you should list any other guaranteed support.

You should state clearly whether or not VAT is included in your calculations.

If you need help in preparing your budget, you should consult an accountant. And if you require advice on VAT then you can obtain information leaflets from your local VAT office. There are also information officers there who can provide advice.

CASE STUDY

Here is a budget for the improvement of ABC's Playground.

Item	**Cost (inc. VAT where applicable) £**
People	
Professional design services	587.50
Project coordinator x 5 days	750.00
Hired facilities	
Hall for public consultation	35.00
Materials	
Playground equipment (includes installation and insurance)	2,500.00

Promotion	
Poster design and print	75.00
Fliers design and print	50.00
Expenses	
Refreshments at public meeting	100.00
Overheads	
Stationery and postage	40.00
Communication support	
(N/a – induction loop in hall)	
Insurance	
(see materials)	
Contingency	100.00
Total	4,237.50

Ready to roll

By now you should have:

1 An audit of potential supporters, identifying people and organisations in a position to help your fundraising.
2 A fundraising strategy reflecting the development plan, and setting priorities and realistic broad action plans to achieve them, making use of the audit of potential supporters.
3 One or more project plan/s providing more information about fundraising priorities and how money will be spent effectively.

Your plans are in place. Now you need to know more about the different sources of funding and we look at some of these in the next few chapters.

CHAPTER 5

Government funding

If you are fundraising on behalf of a school it might receive a certain amount of local education authority funding. This is by no means the only government funding potentially available to schools or to other education organisations.

In this section we look at some of the statutory bodies you could approach. And we provide some general tips on how to request funding.

Some points to bear in mind about statutory funding are:

- public funds normally have strict criteria, fixed deadlines and budget rounds;
- funders require differing degrees of involvement and influence on a project – some enter a contract for a service, others join steering groups, some require an end-of project report;
- funding decisions or programmes can be politically motivated;
- funding themes can change each year;
- often match funding is required;
- bidding in partnership with others can reduce some of the burden of paperwork whilst giving you a stronger case.

Local government

PARISH AND TOWN COUNCILS

At the most local level you might want to work with your parish or town council. They can be a direct source of funds, with a small sum of money to donate each year. Alternatively, they can be helpful supporters of your project in other ways. Parish and town councillors have good networks of contacts and can lobby on your behalf. They also organise regular meetings and can help to promote a specific initiative locally.

CASE STUDY

A small rural primary school received parish council support to upgrade its playground equipment. The parish council made a donation and also secured additional funding from the County Playing Field Association.

LOCAL AUTHORITY OR EDUCATION DEPARTMENT

Your local authority is a good place to begin if you are trying to find out information about available public money.

Your first approach should obviously be to your local education authority, or the education department in your local council. With their experience and overview, they might be able to advise on certain aspects of your project. They may know of some potential sources of funding.

The local education authority makes bids into national government for initiatives such as The Standards Fund in England which, according to the Department for Education and Employment, supports activities which are 'additional to, coherent with, and mutually reinforcing of similar activities funded through other sources such as the Teacher Training Agency INSET funds.'

In the case of The Standards Fund, LEAs bid for money which in some cases is devolved to all relevant schools and in other cases is made available to targeted schools. It can also support council-wide education initiatives. Some grants cover the full costs involved and others offer part-funding. The money is for initiatives such as school improvement and leadership, teacher recruitment, early years work, literacy and numeracy, social inclusion and special needs.

Your local education department might provide you with helpful advice. They can introduce you to other relevant local government departments. They will certainly have details of local and national educational support organisations.

Sometimes a local education department will approach you directly, asking for your help. They might want to set up a community facility using your contacts and physical resources, for example for playschemes, community learning and workshops, etc. These types of projects could bring you in extra money.

The council will also consider requests for capital funding to develop community facilities on more formal education sites. And they will work with you if you want to submit bids for Lottery funding (which is discussed in the next chapter).

CASE STUDY

A secondary school successfully applied to the Sports Lottery Fund for 80 per cent funding towards its £150,000 gymnastics centre. The bid was submitted through the local education department and received additional funding from the council for its new community sports facility.

Occasionally, members of the public donate money directly to an education department. When this happens the education department holds the money on trust and makes it available for suitable educational initiatives outside the core-funded activity.

An LEA might not always provide you with the money you are after, but they may well offer some very helpful free advice.

Other local government departments or agencies might equally be able to provide advice and/or support in kind. They may be willing to set up and run a project in partnership with you. They could have budgets available to support your work.

Below we run through some of the departments or individuals worth approaching. They do not always have the same name or structure in different parts of the UK. And they might operate at county level, within a unitary authority, or within a city, district or borough council. You will need to do a little research to find out the appropriate people in your area. Generally, the *Phone Book* lists local council departments and this will help you with your initial contact. There is also a helpful guide called *The Councils' Handbook* (see Further information, page 122).

ARTS DEVELOPMENT

Many local authorities have arts development officers with a broad remit to support arts and crafts work within the locality. Often the arts budget is more or less committed to ongoing support for major arts organisations, such as theatres, galleries and orchestras. However, arts development officers (ADOs) sometimes have community development or special project budgets. They are also involved in a variety of arts funding networks. And sometimes they are looking for host organisations for funded activities.

So, if you are trying to raise money for an arts project then it is worth consulting your ADO.

CASE STUDY

A small secondary school received project funding from an arts development officer for a crafts partnership with a residential centre for older people. The arts development officer provided the money needed to employ a craftsworker for six day-long sessions, along with a budget for materials and expenses. At the same time the ADO also provided a database of suitable craftworkers, with educational experience, to choose from. The ADO attended each session, providing valuable additional input. The school developed a long-term partnership with the residential centre.

LIBRARIES AND MUSEUMS

Library and museum services are frequently involved in project and outreach work. Sometimes they will have funding available to work on initiatives in partnership with local community groups and schools. On other occasions they will host workshops and externally funded exhibitions. Individual libraries, of course, are an excellent resource for any fundraiser with essential directories of businesses and other reference material freely available.

LEISURE AND TOURISM

Leisure and tourism support and promote local amenities and the area as a whole. It might be worth approaching them if you have a project idea which benefits the wider community and makes your local village or town more attractive to visitors. The leisure and tourism department thrives on creative ideas and is usually quite receptive to appropriate well-planned projects. This department also initiates projects and competitions.

CASE STUDY

A secondary school received £300 prize money in a logo design competition. The prize was awarded by the city council's leisure and tourism department, and the school was free to spend the money on a project of its choice. The competition included activity ideas for teachers to use in the classroom, relating to logo design and branding issues. The £300 prize meant the school hit its fundraising target to set up a circle-time mental health project.

RECYCLING/WASTE MANAGEMENT

Recycling officers often have budgets to develop initiatives with local schools – provided they have an environmental and waste management theme. In addition, recycling officers usually have available some helpful resources on environmental matters, and they can co-ordinate student fact-finding visits to landfill sites and materials recycling facilities.

They might be able to support your environmental project directly, or they might be able to point you to a grant making trust, distributing funds raised through the landfill tax.

COMMUNITY DEVELOPMENT

In the past, many local councils had voluntary sector grant officers with a budget to support community groups. Now it is more common for councils to enter into direct contracts with a number of charities to provide community care services. However, there is usually someone in the council with responsibility for community liaison and development. They might have a grants or development budget. They will certainly have a good network of contacts.

SOCIAL SERVICES

It might be worth approaching your local social services team if you are trying to develop a citizenship project with community partners, such as day care centres or residential homes. They will not always be able to provide direct funding, but they might be able to provide assistance in kind and work with you to raise funds from other sources.

CASE STUDY

A national educational charity works with partner schools and community groups to set up projects which reintegrate young people who have been excluded. Its training, education and employment work is funded by sources including social services, education departments, health authorities, TECs, police and probation.

YOUTH AND COMMUNITY SERVICE

The youth and community service is concerned with informal education. As with social services, it is not very likely that the service will have a budget to provide direct funding. But they might be helpful project partners if you are developing a community sports, health or cultural initiative. They may be able to work with you to secure local authority funding for a joint project. They also have access to wider informal youth funding networks.

ECONOMIC DEVELOPMENT UNITS

Economic development units in most local authorities encourage financial investment in the their area. They also co-ordinate bids for major funding programmes – like the Single Regeneration Budget (SRB) and Agenda 2000 – and work with other agencies to support new and emerging businesses. And they have a wider remit to encourage a coherent and flourishing cultural and economic community.

It is worth enquiring about any partnerships and programmes which your local economic development unit has under way. The unit will be looking for local partners to work directly with the community in different ways. One or more of your proposed projects might be eligible for funding.

If you are not able to apply for direct support there are at least two other ways in which the unit might help.

1 It has a great deal of information about the social and economic climate of the area. This can be helpful background to include in your funding applications.
2 It usually has a detailed directory of businesses based locally. There might be a charge for the directory. It is often available in your local library. Such a directory can be very useful when you are approaching companies for support (see Chapter 7).

CASE STUDY

A home-school association ran an auction of promises to raise money for a 'special olympics' event, bringing together children and families from a number of local special schools.

All the prizes were donated by local businesses, and ranged from a month's subscription to a local gym and a dinner for two, through to a domestic spring clean and four tickets to a football match.

The event organiser had contacted a group of local businesses identified from a directory produced by the local economic development unit. Of the 20 companies approached, 16 provided prizes.

MAYOR'S FUND

Another local source of funding within local government is the mayor's office. Some mayor's funds are focused on one or a handful of chosen local charities. Others are open to applications from groups working in a specific area, such as the environment or young people.

CASE STUDY

An inter-generational education charity successfully applied to their mayor's fund for a grant of £2,500. This sum of money enabled the charity to run a 'cyber family' project providing Internet training and involving three local schools, two pre-schools and three community organisations for older people.

Regional government

REGIONAL GOVERNMENT OFFICES

In England there are ten government offices which act as the regional arms for the Departments of Environment; Trade and Industry; Education; Employment; and Transport. Details of these offices are given in the *Directory of Educational Contacts* (see Further information, page 124). These offices consider the skills and investment needs of their region and include education within their remit.

CASE STUDY

Six schools received funding from a regional government office for projects to raise the career aspirations of teenage girls. The grants were spent on external speakers, materials, exhibitions, staff cover and travel. The funding came from the government office's 'fair play for girls and women' budget.

HEALTH AUTHORITY

Your regional health authority has budgets for health promotion and disease prevention, as well as for care and treatment. Some of this money might be available for community education projects.

Your health authority will have priorities which reflect local need and national targets. If you are planning a project with a health, fitness or lifestyle dimension, then it is worth approaching the health authority.

You will probably find the authority has some helpful resources. And it can introduce you to a wider network of relevant funding organisations.

CASE STUDY

A cluster of local primary and secondary schools formed a 'healthy schools alliance'. One of their first projects focused on World Aids Day, and they began fundraising to set up a community display. Their health authority provided a small grant towards their display materials. The young people produced a series of information sheets and a six foot tall 'Aids ribbon'. The link with the health authority has continued and they have received funding in subsequent years for exhibitions on other health promotion themes.

COMMUNITY PARTNERSHIPS

Local councils and other public bodies play an active role in community partnerships, such as the Single Regeneration Budget, Education Action Zones, Health Action Zones, etc. When approaching a local authority it is worth bearing this in mind. You might be able to become a part of this zone or partnership – helping to give it direction and receiving financial support for some of your community initiatives.

National government funds

Every year new government 'programmes' or initiatives are rolled out. Sometimes they apply throughout the UK, sometimes they are available in particular countries or regions. There are various ways to find out what is available from government departments. There is no single mechanism. Instead it is a case of research at various times during the year and maintaining contacts with relevant organisations. It is worth checking out the various government and quango Websites to find out about new funding programmes. It can also help to subscribe to trade papers and newsletters (such as those produced by your council of voluntary service, or local education authority). Sometimes new funds are promoted through direct mail and you need to contact the department to be put on its mailing list. Other funding initiatives are advertised in national newspapers.

Increasingly government funds are administered by, or channelled through, quangos.

We are going to look at some of these quangos below. But it might be worth mentioning some of the relevant general areas of government which sometimes provide direct project funding, along with useful advice and publications. The structure of national and central government is changing. But there are some general areas which you might consider.

EDUCATION AND EMPLOYMENT

Government is trying to encourage a culture of 'lifelong learning'. Some national funding schemes target specific age ranges or groups of people disadvantaged by their lack of basic skills. Other initiatives are designed to bring different generations together for family learning and mutual benefit.

ENVIRONMENT

The Department for Environment, Transport and the Regions runs initiatives to promote energy efficiency and local action for global change.

HEALTH

The Department of Health is concerned with, amongst other things, health promotion. Much of this work is carried out, under contract, by the Health Education Authority.

CROSS-DEPARTMENT INITIATIVES

There are units – like the Social Exclusion Unit – which work across government departments with a brief to develop partnership initiatives.

Quangos

Over a third of public money is channelled through quangos. And there are about 6,000 such organisations in the UK.

We obviously can't list them all. However, below we highlight some of the quangos that might offer relevant funding opportunities. Some quangos are focused on England and Wales. Others operate throughout the whole UK.

REGIONAL DEVELOPMENT AGENCIES

The regional development agencies look at the needs of a number of counties, grouped together into a region. The RDAs consult with organisations across the region and have responsibility for European Union structural funds. They work on strategic development, with a particular concern for regional competitiveness, and social, physical and economic regeneration. They have funding to invest in public-private partnerships.

REGIONAL ARTS BOARDS

The regional arts boards promote local cultural development and artistic experimentation. They provide funding and spearhead projects which stimulate arts and crafts activities. The RABs encourage the development of new audiences as well as artists.

Some of the RAB officers specialise in particular art forms. There is also usually an education/young people officer.

The RABs offer a variety of grant funding. You might be able to apply for support for a project which fits one of the funding themes. Alternatively, your school might be able to 'host' a project set up by a partner artist or arts organisation.

CASE STUDY

A secondary school worked with a Caribbean writer and theatre director to develop a drama on family conflict and racism. The writer's residency was funded by the regional arts board. It was part of a wider project involving an arts centre and 11 other local schools. Ongoing links were established between a local performance poet, the schools and the arts centre.

TECS AND LECS

Training and Enterprise Councils (TECs) have education departments and try to promote a local learning culture. Your TEC (or LEC – local enterprise council – Scotland's version of TECs) can first of all provide general helpful advice. Your local TEC or LEC will be listed in your *Phone Book*. There is also a TEC National Council (see Further information, page 124). Where funding is concerned, TECs and LECS priorities change to reflect local circumstances and need. Many now devolve a large part of their grant-funding to smaller education-business partnerships.

EDUCATION-BUSINESS PARTNERSHIPS

Education-business partnerships (EBPs) encourage the whole of the local community to be involved in education, in particular businesses. This involvement takes many forms – from providing work experience placements through to acting as one-to-one student mentors. Your local education authority and TEC or LEC will have details of your local education-business partnership (or equivalent organisation). EBPs often have some grant-funding available for specific projects. They have good networks too.

CASE STUDY

An education-business partnership funded a dinner-hour reading project in ten local primary schools. The funding allowed the schools to work with a range of business 'mentors'. Local business people came into school during their lunch break to help pupils with their reading. The financial support covered the initial training and expenses.

HEALTH EDUCATION AUTHORITY

The Health Education Authority (HEA) is a health promotion agency. It has a number of different departments which focus on particular health themes – such as mental health; smoking; and skin cancer (sun awareness). The HEA produces materials, including education resources and posters. It also provides funding for specific initiatives, pilot projects and campaigns.

European initiatives

European funding may be available if you are developing links with other European countries (in a transnational project), if you are working in a geographical area which is recognised as disadvantaged, or if your work supports particular groups of people.

The European Commission administers a number of funding programmes and has vast sums of money to invest. Because there are a number of languages used within the European Union these funding programmes are given neutral names, such as 'Socrates'. New programmes come on stream and names change.

The main community education fund has a budget of several hundred millions of Ecu. In general terms it works to:

- develop a European/intercultural dimension in education and promote improved knowledge of European languages;
- enhance the quality of education through European co-operation and information exchange, the recognition of different qualifications and ways of studying;
- promote mobility of teaching staff and students;
- encourage open and distance learning in the European context.

The European Social Fund is another large source of financial support. Projects supported by the fund need to be broad – with crime reduction, social equity and housing elements, for instance. And the funding must be matched by income from other sources.

You might find that it is helpful to group together with a number of complementary organisations to put together a large joint bid. A sponsoring umbrella organisation could co-ordinate the paperwork and transnational aspects.

There's no denying, though, that applying for European funding is time consuming and heavy on paperwork. The initial research into available grants can also take a lot of effort. Most local authorities have European officers who can advise you on how to proceed, but they often have special areas of interest. They might be unaware of a smaller but specific grant fund which is applicable to you, but they are usually willing to help investigate the opportunities.

You can find information on European funding from your TEC or LEC and on the Web. The Web address is given in Further information, page 128.

General tips

We have seen, then, that there are many different organisations administering and distributing public money. So, it is important to allow yourself time to research potential government funders.

RESEARCH

Once you are absolutely clear about your objectives and the shape of your project, you can search for appropriate sources of funding. You should take into account:

- the scale of your project (is it a small initiative or is it a partnership with a cluster of organisations?);
- the coverage of your project (is it local, regional, national, transnational?);
- the theme/content of your project (is it about regeneration, family learning, cultural diversity, social equity, health?);
- the nature of your project (is it an innovative pilot or is it developing other successful initiatives?);
- the role of your organisation (is your organisation working alone, as a project leader or host, as a partner, under an umbrella?).

Once you have answered these questions you can carry out further research into potential funders.

You also need to consider:

- **eligibility** – of your project and your organisation for their funding;
- **timing** – for applications and project implementation;
- **synergy** – between your respective aims and objectives.

FINDING OUT MORE

Before submitting your proposal you need to find out how the funder wants to be approached. This might be through an application form or a written proposal, limited to a number of sides of A4. Some quangos are now accepting e-mailed applications.

If there isn't an application form to complete, there is usually a set of guidelines. You should ensure you get hold of a copy and follow the instructions. Always obtain the most up-to-date information, as these forms and guidelines are frequently changed or updated.

A contact person is often listed. It is nearly always worth ringing them up for an informal chat. This can give you a clearer idea of what their organisation is looking for. You could ask about past projects that have received funding. You might even tell them briefly about your proposal. In some cases they will be willing to give you some guidance on particular aspects to highlight.

YOUR PROPOSAL

Your project plan will provide you with the basis of your proposal for public funding.

You might need to give more information about your target audience and their needs, along with the potential benefits of your project. Often it is helpful to describe your local area in terms of its social and cultural diversity. This will help to set the context for people who are less familiar with your locality.

Another element which might be additional to your project plan is dissemination (sharing the lessons you have learned with others).

You need to look closely at any guidelines and ensure you have provided all of the information requested. Public funders often ask for measurable targets, so you might need to work out how many people you think your project will help and how you will keep a count.

MATCH FUNDING

It is worth checking whether the fund you are applying to can provide full grant support or only 'match funding'. Grants from government departments and quangos are often for a certain percentage of your total project budget (from 50 to 80 per cent usually). When this is the case contributions in kind can be counted as part of the remaining funding. But some additional money usually has to come in as cash.

Your budget might look like this:

Heading	**Item**	**Cost £**	**Income £**
People:	Speakers	500	
	Co-ordinator	3,000	1,500†
Hired Facilities:	Conference facility	2,500	
Materials:	Delegate packs	1,000	
	Report	500	
Promotion:	Invites	400	
	Newsletter	375	
	Posters	300	
	Business sponsorship	3,000	

† = support provided in kind

In the case of this budget the total costs for your conference amount to £8,575. Your co-ordinator is donating some of their time in kind, which reduces the amount of money you need to raise to £7,075. You have found sponsorship from three local businesses who will exhibit at the conference. In total they are contributing £3,000.

This total leaves you with a fundraising target of £4,075. Some of this might be raised through local events (see Chapter 8); you could for instance raise a further £3,000 in this way. The final £1,075 might be secured from a local charitable trust (see Chapter 6).

Trusts, foundations and the National Lottery

There are about 300 major trusts and foundations in the UK with relatively large funds to distribute. There are also large numbers of smaller trusts, often possessing low levels of income and, therefore, little money to give in grants.

In addition, there are the Lottery distributing bodies which are not officially charitable trusts. They act in a similar way, though, and it is appropriate to use the same general techniques when approaching them.

Some points to bear in mind about trust funding:

- trusts often restrict their funding to registered charities;
- charitable trusts are set up to bring about social change and meet particular needs;
- trust money has been set aside to fund organisations, projects and initiatives;
- trusts recognise the need for small-scale local work as well as large high-profile initiatives;
- you might only be able to secure trust funding for a limited period of time, and you might not be able to re-apply within a certain timescale.

Effective targeting

Trusts and foundations vary enormously. Below we run through just some of the ways in which they differ.

SIZE OF TRUSTS

At one end of the scale there are tiny local family trusts and at the other end there are national foundations with hundreds of staff based in national and regional offices.

MANAGEMENT OF TRUSTS

A part time clerk might be employed to do all the administrative work. Sometimes a firm of accountants or solicitors processes the paperwork. And sometimes trusts employ a number of grant assessors and professional managers.

FUNDING PRIORITIES

The original trust deed defines the focus of a trust's work. The trust might concentrate on specific themes and funding programmes at different times. There are about 200 large charitable trusts providing grants in the area of education (and this excludes the major trust funding strand of medical research).

GRANT MAKING POLICIES

A trust might only provide funding to charities. Alternatively it might support not-for-profit organisations or community groups. Some trusts will only fund groups in a particular geographical area. Others have a maximum and minimum level of donation. Some trusts won't consider funding the same project twice. Some set time limits on the length of projects considered, such as three years.

APPLICATION PROCESSES

Some trusts produce application forms and guidelines and some bodies (like the Sports Council) make electronic application forms available on disk. Many trusts do not outline the information required but wait for requests to come in. Some hold monthly meetings of trustees whilst others hold quarterly or even annual meetings.

LEVELS OF OPENNESS

It is not always easy to work out what a trust is willing to support. Whilst some trusts produce annual reports and detailed funding guidelines, others are quite guarded. There seems to be a fear in some of the smaller trusts that if they are too open about their work they will be overloaded with a flood of relevant applications.

RESEARCHING RELEVANT TRUSTS

From the above it should be clear that there's quite a bit of research to be done if you are hoping to approach a grant making trust.

Helpful directories

Thankfully, there are various resources to help your research, including CAF's *Directory of Grant Making Trusts*, and the Directory of Social Change's *The Education Funding Guide* (see Further information, page 126). Such directories provide useful advice, they index the trusts in various ways and include details such as the trust's main areas of work, levels of grant available, examples of previous grants and contact details.

Working your way through a trust directory can be time-consuming but there is a useful piece of software to help with this process – FunderFinder. Essentially, FunderFinder is a database of trusts with a powerful search mechanism. You key in some of the details of your project and organisation and the package lists a number of appropriate trusts. You can then use this list along with a relevant directory to find out further information.

FunderFinder is available for 'groups in need' and 'people in need'. Prices vary depending on the type of organisation you are: community organisations are charged around £150 initially and then £50 per year to keep the package up to date. Look under FunderFinder in Further information, page 128, for the telephone number to contact if you are interested in this software.

Using this approach you should be able to draw up a shortlist of appropriate trusts and foundations. Some local councils of voluntary service (CVS) are able to give help and guidance in drawing up such a list. You will find their details in your *Phone Book*, or by calling the National Association of Councils of Voluntary Service (see Further information, page 121). The NACVS produces a directory listing affiliated CVSs, but also has details of other developing CVSs.

Further research

Some further research is then needed to confirm that your project and organisation do indeed match up with each trust's funding criteria and priorities. If possible, it is also worth finding out how regularly trustees meet so that you can work out if this fits with your project timetable.

If a trust only considers applications once a year the next meeting might be imminent or months away. You might need to get your project off the ground within a shorter timescale. If this is the case it doesn't matter how well you fit the rest of the criteria, there is no point in making an application.

If a trust provides any further information (over the phone or in a leaflet) then, again, it is worth finding out more. Directories are very helpful, but things inevitably change and the entries become out of date. At the very least you should confirm you have the correct contact address.

It is absolutely essential to research trusts in this way if you are to avoid disappointment and wasted effort. Trust administrators are continually frustrated by inappropriate requests. Many do not even send any sort of reply to mis-directed appeals.

The Foundation for Sport and the Arts

The Foundation for Sport and the Arts (FSA) distributes money provided by the football pool operators. It is distinct from the Lottery distributors. In recent years it has seen its pot of available money shrink quite substantially and secretary to the trustees, Grattan Endicott, says in his guidance notes:

'It is frustrating of course, but our speed of progress is governed by the available money to give away. We do what the unyielding facts allow and we have no way of passing them by. The only remedy is patience.'

The FSA offers grants and interest free loans to create and maintain facilities and opportunities for the general community, or assist sports and arts provision that the community can enjoy.

Two of the areas which are considered and which might be relevant in this context are:

- playgrounds which are for general 'recreational' use (but not those belonging to pre-school playgroups, etc);
- football with strong grassroots or community elements; 'grants will be restricted to local amateur sides, local authority facilities, schools and neighbourhood initiatives' (but such grants are few in number and low in funding levels).

The FSA issues clear guidelines and is completely open about its processes. It provides grants of up to £75,000, likes to be the lead funder or to fund a discrete element of a project, and is sympathetic to applications where groups have already done some degree of community fundraising.

National Lottery distributors

We have already mentioned Lottery distributors as being similar to grant making trusts in many ways. They deserve a little more explanation, though, firstly because they have such large sums of money to distribute regularly and secondly because one particular body, the New Opportunities Fund, prioritises out-of-school hours education and childcare.

The distributors stress that Lottery funding comes from the community and so the resources should be put back into the community. Where schools are involved in bids for Lottery money they need to show that projects aren't eligible for government grant-funding and, importantly, that projects and facilities are for the wider community. They need to work with their local council in putting together a bid. And where building work is involved outline planning permission and other agreements need to be in place.

The relevant Lottery distributors are as follows.

ARTS COUNCILS

Arts Council Lottery funding is available towards the cost of building projects. The arts facilities must be open to the public for a large proportion of the time.

The grants are partnership-funding, so you need to find equal sums from elsewhere. In addition to grants for building and renovation work, a pilot scheme 'Arts 4 Everyone' made project funding available to 'enable more people to attend and participate in arts activity; more new plays, music and other work to be created and promoted to a wider audience.' A successor scheme will operate from April 1999. The contact number is in Further information, page 123, under the Arts Council of England. Your Regional Arts Board can also give you up to date information.

CASE STUDY

A secondary school and sixth form college set up a separate trust to establish an arts centre which would be open to students and available for wider community use. The trust successfully raised the necessary funding from Arts Council Lottery funding, their regional arts board and their local council.

HERITAGE LOTTERY FUND

The Heritage Lottery Fund aims to 'safeguard and enhance the heritage of the United Kingdom. Our heritage encompasses buildings, objects and the environment, whether man-made or natural, which have been important in the formation of the character and identity of the United Kingdom and which will be a vital part of its future.'

The Heritage Lottery Fund (HLF) will consider applications from schools for capital grants, where their land or buildings are considered a real heritage asset, ie they are listed or scheduled. But unlisted buildings in conservation areas are also eligible. Applicants for grants of less than £100,000 need only find partnership funding of ten per cent, while those applying for over £100,000 should find at least 25 per cent partnership funding.

There is also a revenue grants programme, and educational projects with a heritage focus may be eligible. The HLF says on its application form that 'we consider education as one of the most significant aspects of access, and one to which we give high priority, especially where it relates to children and young people.' Contact details are given in Further information, page 123.

CASE STUDY

A conservation trust received from the Heritage Lottery Fund nearly half the funds needed to set up an educational programme based on the natural and industrial heritage of a local river. The project is being run in partnership with local primary schools and focuses on the environmental and expressive arts within the curriculum.

NATIONAL LOTTERY CHARITIES BOARD

The National Lottery Charities Board does not provide grants directly to schools at the moment, unless there are exceptional circumstances. Grants are given to help those at greatest disadvantage and to improve the quality of life of the community. Pre-school organisations have, however, successfully applied for NLCB funding, and other educational initiatives have been supported where the project co-ordinators are community or charitable organisations. The contact number is given in Further information, page 123.

CASE STUDY

Two neighbouring pre-schools received grants under the NLCB's Community Involvement programme. One was awarded over £8,000 and the other nearly £4,000 so that they could expand the support offered to local children with special educational needs.

SPORTS COUNCILS

The Sports Council, like the Arts Council, part-funds capital projects. The sports facilities must be available to the general public for a large part of the time. One of the elements within the capital facility programme encourages 'sporting partnerships between schools and the community'.

There are also awards for individuals and projects under themes such as 'coaching and leadership' and 'talent identification'. The contact numbers are given in Further information, page 123.

THE MILLENNIUM COMMISSION

The Millennium Commission has made most of its large grants, and funding may be available through organisations who have received grants to distribute to community groups.

AWARDS FOR ALL

All the Lottery distributors jointly consider small grants to small organisations through 'Awards for All'.

THE NEW OPPORTUNITIES FUND

The New Opportunities Fund provides support to a variety of community-partnership initiatives, including out of school hours activities. Under the out of school hours activities heading there are two main priorities – study support and childcare.

Each study support project should include at least one of the schools served by the project (possibly in partnership with the voluntary sector, local authority and local businesses, or in a cluster with several other schools).

An out of school hours childcare project might involve one or more schools, community groups, local authorities, playgroups or private sector providers.

The aim of study support initiatives, according to the Secretary of State, should be to 'complement and support the work of teachers in the classroom... creating well motivated, independent young people who will become lifelong learners.' Examples of such activities include:

- homework clubs;
- mentoring;
- drama;
- creative and sporting activities;
- community service.

Kids' Club Network

Kids' Club Network provides valuable advice and publications on setting up an after school club and on raising money from a variety of sources, including the New Opportunities Fund. In addition, it runs a quality assurance scheme, training and a special information line. Contact details are included in Further information, page 126.

THE NATIONAL ENDOWMENT FOR SCIENCE, TECHNOLOGY AND THE ARTS

The National Endowment for Science, Technology and the Arts (NESTA) was established in July 1998 to support and promote talent, innovation and creativity in the fields of science, technology and the arts. The focus is on support for individuals so that they can achieve their potential. NESTA says that it 'intends to be flexible and imaginative and offer effective solutions to developing individuals and to freeing them from impediment to achieve their potential.'

NESTA was provided with an endowment of £200 million from the National Lottery. It spends money which is raised from the interest on this endowment (around £10 to £12 million per year). As well as funding individuals, it might consider funding masterclasses and centres of excellence. Contact details are given in Further information, page 122.

Dormant trusts and community foundations

When you are researching appropriate trusts it is worth considering two particular types of organisation – dormant trusts and community foundations.

There are a number of dormant family trusts which are looked after by firms of solicitors and which can't be closed until the money is distributed. Often educational projects are eligible for funding. So, if you have some old firms of solicitors in your area it is worth a quick enquiry to see if they are overseeing such funds.

Community foundations fundraise to support projects and facilities within a particular local area. Your local authority or council of voluntary service will probably know if there is a community foundation in your area or contact The Association of Community Trusts and Foundations (ACTAF), see Further information, page 122.

Tailor-made proposals

Grant making trusts and similar bodies work in very different ways and offer support to a wide range of organisations and initiatives.

If possible, you should try to make contact with the trust before you put together an application for funding. This won't always be possible. But speaking over the phone, or meeting up with a trustee or administrator, can reveal the 'personality' of the organisation. It is through this kind of contact that you can start to develop a relationship with the trust.

Such a relationship is important because it means the trust will know something about your work and you will have a certain amount of credibility; you won't be cold-calling.

APPROACHING TRUSTS ON THEIR TERMS

Every formal approach to a trust should be on their terms. This doesn't mean that you should invent a new project or skew your scheme so that it fits their priorities. Instead, it means that you should:

- set out your application in the format they prefer (if, indeed, they state a preference);
- draw attention to the way in which your project benefits the people they want to help (their target group);
- highlight the ways in which your project reflects their policies and purposes;
- describe things in their language (you might use phrases like 'capacity building' and 'lifelong learning' to help them see how your work is relevant to their aims);
- apply for appropriate levels of funding and for relevant elements – if you are providing a full project budget but only requesting a grant towards part of the money needed, make this clear;
- ensure you include all the information they ask for – if you miss something out this will at the very least delay the whole process and at worst the trust might rule out your application altogether.

YOUR LETTER

If the trust doesn't have an application form, then you will need to write a letter applying for funding. This shouldn't be a mail-merged document where you simply change the name and address at the top of the page and follow it with a standard appeal letter. It should be personalised and punchy, briefly summarising your application and saying why you are applying to that trust.

You might want to contain all relevant details within a letter of up to two pages. Alternatively you might want to send a short letter accompanied by a one or two page proposal. All letters and proposals should be word-processed or typed and presented clearly and neatly.

YOUR PROPOSAL

Your proposal should be a readable and persuasive document. Avoid pleas which involve talk about being 'desperate for funding'. Instead, you should be positive and enthusiastic.

Your opening paragraph should say:

1 why there is a need for the project;
2 how your work can make a difference, and
3 how much money you are requesting.

Make it read like the first lines of a newspaper report. If the reader put your proposal down at this point they should understand the essence of your application. You are aiming to grab their attention so that they will want to continue.

Now you can outline your plans in more detail. It is helpful to present this as small chunks of information punctuated with headings. This enables the trust to find their way around your application easily. It will also help you to remain concise and relevant.

Within the proposal you might describe:

Your target audience/beneficiaries

It is important to show how your work will make an impact on people and communities. Your target audience might exactly match the trust's priorities or might be a 'sub-set'. So, for instance, a trust might support work with young people, and your project might be aimed at disadvantaged young people.

User involvement/consultation process

The people who benefit from a community project should be fully involved in the development and running of the project. Some funders describe this as 'user involvement'. And if people can't be actively involved, they should be given the opportunity to put their views forward through ongoing consultation and representation.

Needs, aims and objectives and benefits

Charitable trusts generally invest money in projects which meet a social need and make a difference to people's lives. So it is important to outline the need for your project, citing any evidence you have to support this claim. If you have done a pilot project (a small scale test of your project) then include details of who participated, why and what they thought about the possibility of such work on a larger scale. Letters of support can be useful.

Once you have said what the need is, explain how your project can meet this need. State the aims and objectives of the project and list the benefits to all involved.

Work involved/methodology

You might have worthwhile aims, but can you actually achieve what you set out to do? A trust will want to be confident that you have the ability to deliver the project effectively. And one way to reassure them is to briefly explain how you will carry out the work. Try not to get bogged down in a detailed workplan, but give general headings about the type of work involved, the people who will work on various aspects of the project and the broad timetable. This section should show that you have a good understanding of what's involved and you are planning in a realistic way.

Quality control and equal opportunities

In this section you should outline your commitment to the quality of your project (through monitoring and evaluation).

You should also say how you will apply your equal opportunities policy in this particular project.

Other funders

Trusts don't usually mind contributing to a project alongside a variety of other funders. Often their grants are limited and can't make up the full sum of money you are looking for. So, you need to include a section in your proposal which says how you hope to secure all the income you need. You might have raised some money from individuals. Some organisations might have already guaranteed their contribution. Your own organisation might have some general funds to commit to the project. You should include all of this information, along with details of other potential sources (such as match funding from a government scheme, for instance).

And if you want your project to continue after the initial grant-funding has run out, then you need to say how you plan to achieve this.

Again, it all helps to reassure a potential funder that you have planned properly and that their money will achieve things if it is put into your project.

Sustainability/exit strategy

In this section you need to say what you plan to do when the money runs out. How will the project carry on once established? Is it a one-off initiative? Will someone else fund it or carry it forward? You need to look to the longer term and reassure a potential funder that you won't be coming back in three years time asking for help so that the project doesn't collapse.

WOULD YOU FUND YOUR PROJECT?

When you read through your proposal you should be able to say: 'That sounds good. I'd fund that.'

Now, think about the organisation you are approaching. Taking account of their funding priorities and any guidelines they produce, how will they react? Will they read your proposal and say: 'That's just the sort of thing we're looking for?'

Supporting documentation

Once you have a brief, relevant and persuasive proposal you are almost ready to send it off. However, it is important to give your proposal credibility. You need to attach a variety of supporting documentation.

MORE ABOUT THE PROJECT

You might want to include the full project plan if this goes into a lot more detail. It is also worth including relevant research documents or extracts from them to give evidence of the need for your project.

The detailed budget will be included in your project plan. But you might want to highlight any elements which are already funded. Or you might outline the next steps in your fundraising strategy to secure the full budget.

MORE ABOUT YOUR ORGANISATION

It can be helpful to enclose your organisation's development plan, showing the general direction your organisation is moving in. Trusts will want to know more about how long you have been operating, your size and your constitution.

It is also useful to enclose information on some of the people who will carry out work on the project.

FINANCIAL BACKGROUND

Trusts usually ask for copies of your organisation's last available audited accounts and annual report. Some also ask to see your annual budget. This helps them to get a feel for the overall scope and scale of your work.

CHAPTER 7

Corporate support

In the last chapter we looked at charitable trusts and foundations. These organisations are focused on meeting needs and improving people's lives. Businesses exist to make a profit. Why, then, would they give their money away to support education?

There are many reasons why a business donates money or offers sponsorship to a community cause or organisation. We explore some of the reasons in this section, and we look at the different types of support on offer to schools and community education projects.

Some points to bear in mind about corporate funding:

- companies don't have to give money to community causes;
- some companies which support community projects are reluctant to support schools and educational initiatives;
- most medium and large firms have a policy on community giving and will be happy to send out details on this to prevent inappropriate approaches;
- there is a distinction between corporate sponsorship and donations: sponsorship money is given in return for branding and association with the project or cause and VAT is payable – donations are made with no strings attached and VAT is not payable;
- personal links with companies can help you to get in contact with the right people and to convince them that your organisation is sound and your project likely to be successful;
- if you buy products and services from companies, then you can encourage your suppliers to fundraise for you or to make a contribution to your appeal (this is called 'facilitated giving');
- companies have a variety of reasons for supporting educational projects and you need to show how your project fits within their policy (without compromising it).

The Confederation of British Industry (CBI) believes that 'without an effective partnership between businesses and education, the prospects for an internationally competitive UK economy in the 21st century will become remote.' (CBI report: *Building a Stronger Partnership Between Business and Education*).

What is a company looking for?

Every company will have its own policy on support for schools and community groups. At its most basic this might be:

- we don't make any donations, there's not enough cash; or
- the managing director makes discretionary decisions about donations.

You aren't going to get very far with either sort of business unless you have good contacts with the managing director!

Other companies are more positive and proactive when it comes to community involvement.

- Some companies channel their support through sponsorship (where the company gives money for a high profile association with a project – they pay for the value of this branding which can be more than the cost of the project).
- Some companies make donations (where the company gives money to a community project, covering specific costs, and receives some credit for involvement).
- Other companies provide both kinds of support through different community or corporate involvement programmes.

We talk about the distinction between sponsorship and donations in more detail below. But let's look at some of the general reasons for business giving.

COMMUNITY RELATIONS

Many companies recognise they have an impact on the community in which they are based. This impact might be mainly on the immediate area around each of their premises, or might be more general if they sell goods and services nationwide. The impact ranges from an increase in traffic and noise through to providing local employment and stimulating the creation of smaller supply companies.

In some cases businesses want to put something back into the community to balance the negative effects of their work. In other instances, they want to create goodwill or generally be a good neighbour. Sometimes, they are hoping to develop new or stronger links with local community groups – perhaps because they want support for (or few objections to) a planning application, for instance.

National businesses are interested in developing and maintaining loyalty amongst local people. Many local branches of national retailers, for instance, have their own devolved community affairs budget.

Some companies believe they have a straightforward role as a 'philanthropist'. They are a big player in the local community and work with relatively large sums of money. As one of the few organisations who can make a difference they believe they should. The charity 'Include' says: 'healthy businesses need healthy communities and it is the duty of businesses to work for social inclusion.'

SOCIAL INVESTMENT

Companies might have a strong connection with a particular cause, or they might adopt a particular theme. They might choose to support various projects which help disabled people, or which combat crime, for instance.

CASE STUDY

A high street bank set up a project to support educational initiatives with a financial theme. Funding and resource materials were made available. Schools and community groups applied for funding to set up commerce projects. It was in the bank's interest to develop the financial literacy of young people. At the same time schools needed extra funding to set up valuable work-related events.

CASE STUDY

An insurance company focused its community support on carers' projects. Funding was given to schools which set up support groups and peer-counselling for young carers. The company also funded an education resource which was produced by a partnership involving the local education authority, carers' groups and schools. As well as providing the funding required to produce the resource, the company helped with publicity and postage of packs to those organisations across the UK who requested copies.

COMPETITION

Some companies are a little more cynical or, at least, pragmatic. Their competitors are involved in community and educational initiatives. They need to keep up with this competition, showing customers and staff that they are just as involved in the community. They get involved because it is expected of them. Such companies are unlikely to have sophisticated funding policies.

EMPLOYEE RELATIONS

A company's staff are generally drawn from the local community. When a firm puts money into community projects then these often involve or concern staff and their families. This support can boost staff morale and commitment to the company.

Further, some companies encourage employee involvement in the local community by providing match funding for their work; others offer time off or secondments; and others provide help in kind. Businesses recognise the benefits for their employees' personal development through voluntary work.

CASE STUDY

A national business encourages its staff to volunteer as school governors, where they have the appropriate skills. It does this through internal information campaigns and training workshops. Staff who are governors are entitled to the equivalent of three working days off in lieu each year to allow them to attend governor meetings and events. The company says that it runs this initiative to 'develop the communications and planning skills of our staff, and to support employees and their families in a direct and visible way.'

PUBLIC RELATIONS

Public relations and promotional activities help to get more people involved in a project – attending events, volunteering their time, etc. But a business usually wants additional PR; either to highlight its generosity or to draw attention to a specific product or service.

When the coverage is limited to a cheque presentation enabling the project to go ahead then this is regarded as a donation. If a company starts to create a strong link between its firm or a brand and the organisation or project then this becomes sponsorship. It is important to know the difference because there are tax implications – VAT is payable on sponsorship but not on donations.

Marketing

A company's marketing department might be interested in reaching a particular group of people (potential customers). If your project hits just the right target audience, then this might interest them. Equally, if support for an educational project gives them an edge over their competitors, then this might prompt their involvement.

They might even launch an initiative that benefits you and at the same time increases their sales. This technique (cause-related marketing) has been used by a number of supermarkets, often linking with an educational cause.

Customers are issued with points or tokens which can be redeemed by local schools in exchange for computers and other resources. The schools ask parents to donate their tokens – encouraging people indirectly to shop in a particular store. Such schemes can provide schools with valuable resources. But, while you need to flag up the opportunity to parents, you need to take care not to make them feel pressurised to shop in a particular store or to buy more than they would normally.

KEY OPINION FORMERS

There are a number of people who are regarded by companies as significant 'key opinion formers'. They might be buyers for other firms if the company is involved in selling to other businesses. They might be politicians at local, national or European level. Companies want to show them that they are responsible and active in the community. Ultimately, they want these people's goodwill and support.

Who to approach

We have seen, then, that companies support community projects for a variety of different reasons. Not all provide help to educational initiatives. To save a lot of misdirected and wasted effort, you should spend some time researching appropriate companies and then who to approach within them.

IDENTIFYING RELEVANT COMPANIES

It is worth holding a brainstorming session and building up a list of potential company funders. This can then be refined into a database as you find out more information about each company.

Various people and organisations can give you leads and ideas. The following are potential sources of information and connections:

- staff (family, friends and knowledge of parents, etc);
- parents (own companies and contacts);
- governors/board/committee members;
- business suppliers;
- business link organisations – these provide a one-stop shop for county-wide business support services, including enterprise agencies and location authorities – such organisations are listed in your *Phone Book*;
- chamber of commerce;
- education-business partnership;
- TEC/LEC;
- local education authority;
- economic development unit (in your local council);
- *Yellow Pages* and business directories;
- and finally, Business in the Community, an organisation which is an important source of relevant information (see Further information, page 123, for the contact details).

APPROPRIATE DEPARTMENTS WITHIN COMPANIES

Once you have names and contact details for a number of companies it is time to do some further research into the relevant departments and their funding policies.

In smaller companies the managing director might make all decisions on donations and sponsorship. The firm might ask for requests to be sent to the managing director, their personal assistant or to some other nominated board member.

In medium-sized companies or larger firms you might find different individuals or different departments dealing with funding requests. Unfortunately a request sent inappropriately to the personnel department might simply be turned down and not passed on to another interested department.

CASE STUDY

A community education group contacted a large bank to request support for a student resource focusing on age and disability awareness. The group sent its proposal to the bank's corporate relations department which turned it down. At a later date the group discovered that the human resources team within the same bank had a budget to develop equal opportunities initiatives in the local community. The group submitted its proposal again, to the head office of the same bank. This time its approach was successful.

The different departments which might have a budget to support your project include:

- corporate relations;
- community affairs;
- marketing;
- sponsorship;
- public relations;
- human resources;
- personnel;
- training and development.

How to make your approach

You should make your initial enquiries over the phone to establish:

1. that there is a budget to support your sort of project;
2. which department holds this budget;
3. the contact name of the person in charge of the budget (with the correct spelling of their name and their title);
4. any details of the funding cycle and timetable;
5. how they prefer to be approached – are they open to a preliminary meeting or phone call, for instance, or would they like to receive a written proposal?

Most companies expect to receive a funding request in writing. This should take the form of a brief covering letter with your proposal enclosed. The proposal should be short – about two or three sides of A4.

In the covering letter you might mention any past contact you have had with the firm. You might refer to more recent conversations with members of staff or other important contacts you know. This all helps to personalise your approach, showing that you haven't just picked their company at random.

The covering letter should excite and enthuse, making the reader want to delve into the accompanying proposal. So, you should say why you are approaching their particular company. And you should sum up your project in no more than three punchy sentences.

Trusts and statutory funders often want to see background papers giving evidence of need and financial information about your organisation when they consider your request. Companies usually prefer to receive less paperwork at the outset. Some go on to ask for more background as your proposal is processed. Others, however, will consider your proposal as it stands. Occasionally it might be appropriate to enclose a photograph or illustration, depending on what you are proposing.

The proposal document will vary depending on who you are approaching and what sort of funding you are going for – sponsorship or donation.

ELEMENTS OF A PROPOSAL DOCUMENT

Some of the common elements will be as follows.

Introduction to your organisation

A quick description of who you are, what you do and how you are funded. Mention other successful initiatives.

Introduction to the project

In this section you should outline:

- the need for the project and its value;
- what you are trying to achieve;
- what makes the project is special or unique.

If you can look outwards at some trend or issue that makes your proposal topical, then it is worth mentioning this to give it a context.

Project participants and beneficiaries

Here you outline who will be involved and who will benefit from the project, how you will reach them and what they will gain. If the company identifies a target group in its funding policy then your description should fit within this category. It is worth spelling this out if possible.

What is involved

In this section you will give a bit more information about how the project will work in practice, with indicative timings.

Costings/funding request

If you are applying for a donation then you should outline the costs of the project and explain what sum you are requesting. If you are asking for sponsorship then you don't need to provide the full costings, you attach a value to the elements you are offering for sponsorship and state the fee.

Benefits

If this is a sponsorship proposal, then you need to identify the benefits to the sponsor (see below). The benefits should be adapted in each proposal to reflect the interests of the potential sponsor you are approaching.

Types of contribution

Companies can support educational groups in a variety of ways – financially and with resources. Below we look at some of the different things which you might ask for.

DONATIONS

A donation is a financial contribution with no strings attached and, as we have mentioned earlier, no VAT payable. The donor shouldn't ask for lots of branding or for high profile photo opportunities.

In other words, it isn't a commercial transaction where the company is buying an association with your organisation or project. It is providing the money because it likes your work and it fits in with its grant-giving policy.

When you approach a company for a donation, you should send an appropriate proposal. This should contain full project costings and be quite similar in tone to an approach to a trust or foundation. In fact, a number of companies have set up associated charitable trusts to make donations.

Another way of securing donations can be through a staff funding scheme. Companies might run such a scheme alongside their other community support. They might channel all their funding to projects involving employees. In this sort of scheme the staff make an application on behalf of a community project in which they are involved. Some companies offer to match any funding their employee raises from other sources. Others consider straightforward proposals presented by members of staff.

CASE STUDY

A regional company provides donations to community groups through an associated charitable trust. Alongside the open opportunity for all local groups to apply, there is a staff scheme. Each month employees can nominate groups for consideration. Staff have to show that they are actively involved in the group's work.

CASE STUDY

A nursery group received £2,000 to pay for an information technology project run in partnership with the Women's Institute. The employee was involved in the WI. So, the nursery managed to raise the funds because someone working voluntarily for the partner organisation also worked for a company with a staff donation policy. The successful result was worth all the research involved in making the connections!

SPONSORSHIP

Sponsorship, by contrast, is definitely a commercial transaction. A company wants to gain from its association with your work or cause. You are charging for this association – and you might put a value on such sponsorship which is ten times the actual project cost.

You need to be realistic, though, and compare what you are offering with other competing sponsorship opportunities, advertising and alternative promotional activities. This is what a potential sponsor will do. So, you need to stress the benefits and opportunities in your proposal.

Such benefits might include:

- association with a particular issue or cause;
- improved community relations;
- opportunity for staff involvement and development;
- promotional opportunities for services and products;
- opportunity to meet key decision makers.

You also need to say how the sponsor will gain profile through, for instance:

- branding and credits (on materials, on signs, on letterhead);
- involvement in a launch event;
- publicity (media coverage, advertising, posters).

CASE STUDY

An educational music organisation wanted to run a training event for teachers and community music workers. The event was costed at £3,000. A charitable trust donated a grant of £2,000. Income from tickets sold to 100 delegates at £10 each provided the remaining funding required. During the event delegates said it would be helpful to have a regional directory of important organisations and individuals. The original income from the grant, and from ticket sales, had all been spent on the cost of the event and the production and dissemination of the directory would cost a further £1,000. The organisation could have gone back to their trust funder to see if any additional donation was available. However, they felt that the directory provided a sponsorship opportunity worth twice the direct costs. They approached a number of regional companies requesting £2,000 in sponsorship and found two companies willing to co-sponsor the directory.

Once you have secured an offer of sponsorship it is very important to have a written agreement. You can write a letter saying thank you for the offer and reiterating what has been agreed. Alternatively the company might send you a letter or contract.

IN KIND SUPPORT

Some companies offer in kind support alongside financial help. Others, who have no funding or donations budget, are still able to provide help in kind. This help involves providing goods or services at no cost. In some cases this is the firm's main line of business – such as plumbing or accountancy.

In other instances, support will involve the donation of an item of equipment like a computer, or the provision of free office accommodation for a project worker. Many large companies replace equipment at regular three to five year intervals; this equipment ranges from computers through to desks and chairs and is often available for donation.

There are three further areas of in kind support that might be helpful.

People and advice

Some firms are willing to second staff to help community and educational organisations. They see the experience as a valuable element of staff development. When secondees are matched with appropriate opportunities this can be very beneficial for all involved. Unfortunately, staff are sometimes seconded because they are not doing well at their jobs but are too expensive to make redundant. It is therefore important to draw up a detailed job description and ensure the secondee has the necessary skills and experience.

CASE STUDY

A pre-school playgroup worked with a seconded business manager to develop a business plan and training programme for volunteers. The business manager completed her time with the group and returned to her original job. She also continued to fundraise for the pre-school as a volunteer.

An alternative to a straightforward secondment is a job-swap for a limited time. For a short period, a worker from your organisation takes up a role in a company. The person in that post comes to work in your organisation. Again, preparation is vital and the right people need to be involved. You can gain new ideas, a fresh and challenging perspective and a new understanding of the way different sectors work. Job shadowing (sitting alongside someone as they do their work) can provide similar opportunities.

Companies can be a good source of advice and training. They might not have funding to support you directly, but they could be prepared to give up some time to advise you on management issues, such as marketing or recruitment. Occasionally a company might have a training course with vacant delegate places. They might offer you the chance to attend. To find out about this sort of opportunity you usually need to have an established relationship with the firm.

Finally, local businesses can help you to recruit governors or management committee members. They can promote the opportunity and benefits to staff and support them with time off in lieu to attend meetings.

Opening up the world of work

Links with a company offer other benefits to the young people you are working with. There might be the chance to provide some work experience, educational visits or relevant careers advice. Companies sometimes offer a member of staff to give a talk or to participate in a business event for young people.

Educational resources

Another area to consider is free or subsidised educational resources. A number of companies create relevant materials. Some are designed to be used within the curriculum. Others are more general in their application.

Such resources obviously need to be handled carefully to ensure that they are balanced, well-researched and meet a genuine education need. If they are of sufficient quality then they can be a valuable enhancement.

National Consumer Council guidelines

The National Consumer Council has produced guidelines on *Sponsorship in Schools*. The guidelines contain some helpful advice for all educational organisations involved in some way with external sponsorship (see Further information, page 121, for the contact address).

There are guidelines for the producers and promoters of sponsored activities. And on behalf of the recipient the NCC suggests you ask the following questions:

- is it clear who the sponsor/producer is?
- does its educational value outweigh its marketing messages?
- is the approach to the subject balanced and up to date?
- is it relevant to the curriculum and age group?
- has it been tested for use in schools?
- is it free of stereotypes?
- can children and teachers participate without buying the sponsor's products?
- is it free of messages that encourage children to pester adults about buying a specific firm's products or services?
- is it free of incentives to children to eat an unhealthy diet or take part in unsafe or unhealthy activities?
- are the benefits of the sponsored offer worthwhile and achievable?

Give as You Earn

Give As You Earn (GAYE), a form of payroll giving, is another way to involve companies in your fundraising. Essentially you are asking individuals to donate a sum of money out of their salary on a regular basis. GAYE offers a tax-efficient way of achieving this. The company needs to agree to set up the opportunity and possibly promote its availability to staff.

To benefit from payroll giving your organisation must be a charity. This method of fundraising is not currently widely used by educational organisations. For more information contact the Charities Aid Foundation.

Building a relationship

If you are successful in securing help of any kind from a company then you should view this as something to build on. Even if you manage to raise thousands of pounds from one firm this shouldn't be the end of the matter. At the very least you should keep your supporters informed and thank them publicly.

Ideally, you should aim to develop an ongoing relationship with them – ring them up with news, send them newsletters and literature, invite them to events and involve them where you can.

When you establish a good relationship with a company you:

- are kept up to date with emerging funding opportunities;
- have credibility and a 'warm lead' if you need to approach them for further support;
- make them feel good about the help they have provided;
- create the possibility that they will offer to support a new project even before you ask for help!

All of these things apply to every funder and we'll return to this in Chapter 10. In the next chapter, though, we are going to look at fundraising from the local community.

CHAPTER 8

Community fundraising

In the past, most voluntary funding for education came from individuals and small neighbourhood associations. Raising money in this way can be quite labour intensive. It is still worth doing, though, to develop stronger community relationships and to involve people locally in your work. It is also a useful demonstration to funding organisations that you have made an effort to raise money locally.

Community organisations

Community fundraising concentrates on raising money from local people as individuals and families. But there are some groups and associations at a community level which you should consider, because they might raise money for you.

Such organisations worth thinking about in this way, are as follows.

BUSINESS AND PROFESSIONAL CLUBS

Many local business people and retired professionals meet for pleasure and learning in some sort of club. The club raises money from members and others for specific causes or organisations. It is worth talking to your equivalent of the Round Table, Rotary or Lions club to find out if one of your initiatives is of interest.

WOMEN'S INSTITUTE OR MOTHERS UNION

Organisations such as the WI are also worth involving in your community fundraising. They might put on fundraising talks and events on your behalf.

They could work in partnership with you to provide some practical support for fundraising events. If you are working together then it is important to make it a two-way exchange – find out what their members might want to gain from the partnership.

COMMUNITY STORE/LOCAL PUB

A local shop or pub can help with your community fundraising. They may be willing to promote your fundraising events. They could be interested in actively raising money on your behalf through pub quizzes, for instance.

CASE STUDY

A rural pub raised £500 for the village primary school through a pub quiz night. At the same time its takings for the night rose by 50 per cent.

CASE STUDY

A special school needed to raise £40,000 for a new sports hall. The school made an appeal for help to the local pub and 30 regulars agreed to go on a sponsored bike ride. This raised the first £10,000 of the money required.

Collections

It is unlikely that you are going to set up a house-to-house collection of money for your educational project. But there are important rules to be aware of, if you are thinking of collecting jumble or aluminium cans, for instance, to raise money.

A 'collection' might involve standing on a street corner with a collecting tin, but it goes much wider than this. It covers not only appeals for money, but also jumble, recyclables, etc along with offers of goods or services for payment in a public place or by making visits from place to place (eg to people's homes).

Anyone making such a collection must be at least 16 years old. All collectors have to have official badges and written authority for their involvement (possibly a certificate). The organisation concerned must have a permit from the local council. The only exceptions are: collections in a place of worship, appeals made during a meeting, and an unattended collection container.

Events

Events are often exhausting and nerve racking for the organisers; they can be pleasurable for those attending or taking part, but they are not generally big moneyspinners.

Events require careful planning and the organisers need clearly defined roles. You should prepare a detailed timetable with weekly actions to be completed to meet your deadlines.

You also need to have a date agreed for reviewing the responses (if it is a ticketed event) and it is on this date that you decide whether or not to go ahead.

Below is an organiser's checklist which you might want to adapt for your particular event:

- set ideal date and agree type of event;
- agree cut-off point to assess responses and give go-ahead for event;
- agree roles and responsibilities;
- plan broad content of event;
- set venue criteria (including access for disabled delegates);
- research and identify appropriate venue;
- draft invitations and promotional materials;
- design and print literature;
- begin promotion;
- book speakers/entertainers/exhibitors;
- invite VIPs;
- hire equipment, including microphones;
- take out relevant insurance;
- agree catering and refreshment arrangements;

- health and safety checklist and arrangements;
- press and publicity;
- re-confirm all arrangements and brief participants;
- prepare signs for venue;
- brief all helpers;
- prepare name badges;
- evaluate.

You will see from the above checklist that one of your first decisions needs to be the type of event to hold. Perhaps you hold an annual fete and an annual jumble sale. Two or three events in a year is about as much as the local community will stand. You might make subtle changes to your standard events at first, or introduce new elements. You might have a third event which is a little more daring. Or you could do something different each year.

Here are some of the many different community fundraising event options:

- auction – of promises, of celebrity items/signatures;
- boat race;
- community play;
- dance workshop;
- exhibition – of local arts and crafts;
- fashion show;
- gallery trail (arts exhibits throughout the community in people's homes);
- highland games;
- inside out party (where you wear your clothes inside out);
- jigsaw giant (a marathon jigsaw event covering a large area with many jigsaws);
- karaoke;
- local olympics;
- murder mystery event;
- nun run (like a fun run in costume);
- open air concert;
- pantomime;
- quiz;

- rumble in the jumble (same old thing new name!);
- safari supper (at various venues for each course);
- treasure hunt;
- under fives talent show;
- Valentine Ball;
- Christmas Fair;
- youth festival;
- zany day (during which people can participate in a series of unusual activities like custard pie fights, gunge baths, etc).

If you are thinking of running an event, you can obtain a free copy of a leaflet called *How to Sleep at Night* from the ICFM (see Further information, page 127). You could also consult the CAF How To… guide *Organising a Millenium Event*.

Legal issues

PUBLIC ENTERTAINMENT LICENCE

If you are putting on an event which is open to all members of the public who want to attend and you are providing some entertainment – from music and dancing to drama and sports – then you will probably need a venue with a public entertainment licence. Most secondary schools have such licences already. Community centres and village halls often have them too.

If a venue doesn't have such a licence then you'll need to apply to the local authority for one, and this takes time. The council will look to see that you have adequate fire precautions, toilets, kitchens and facilities for hand-washing.

Even if a venue has a licence you need to remember that if your event leads to complaints about, for instance, noise then that licence may be jeopardised. It wouldn't do much good for your relationship with a school if you lost them their public entertainment licence in the course of running a fundraising event for them!

LICENCE TO SELL ALCOHOL

If you are running an event for people aged 18 and over then you might want to provide a bar. This must be licensed. You need to allow at least eight weeks to make such an application and it can be much easier to invite a local publican in if they have the appropriate licence.

HEALTH AND SAFETY MATTERS

You might want to devise a health and safety checklist to ensure everything is in order. Your local authority can provide guidelines.

Things to consider include:

- first aid – you might want to involve the St John Ambulance or British Red Cross;
- facilities and equipment;
- food and drink hygiene;
- insurance;
- parking;
- smoking (or smoking ban).

COPYRIGHT

When people put on a play they often leave issues connected with royalties and copyright until the last minute. This is a dangerous tactic because permission for performance can be refused. A work comes out of copyright 70 years after it was first published or recorded. You will find details of who you need to contact for permission to perform a play on the script. This permission often has conditions (for instance, that you are not allowed to record the performance).

You also need to consider the performance of music and you should contact the Performing Rights Society for advice.

CASE STUDY

A secondary school had rehearsed its play for months and was putting on the performance to raise money for its own needs and for a local hospice. Unfortunately, the relevant permission wasn't sought until two weeks before the performance. Permission was refused because a national theatre company had just begun a tour and was coming to the area. The school's performance could be seen as being in direct competition. Despite national media coverage the school play had to be cancelled.

INSURANCE

If you are organising an event in a school building then it is worth checking with the LEA (if appropriate) to see if anything is covered.

If you are taking out insurance then things to consider include:

- weather;
- accidents;
- hired equipment;
- public liability;
- employers' liability;
- theft.

Games of chance and competitions

Raffles, draws and lotteries are games of chance. Tickets are sold and the ticket holder could win a prize or cash. These activities are a form of gambling and are covered by the National Lottery Act 1993 and the Lotteries Regulations 1993.

The law defines three main types of lotteries and there are rules and regulations depending on the type you are planning.

Below we provide a brief summary of the three types of lotteries, but you should check with your local authority or with a solicitor if you are in any doubt about what you are planning.

There are fines of up to £5,000 if you commit a minor offence and more substantial fines with prison sentences if you commit a serious offence.

SMALL LOTTERIES

A small lottery is a draw or raffle which takes place during an entertainment event – such as a ball or fête. People shouldn't attend just to take part in the draw, they should come along for the other main attraction.

You mustn't spend more than £250 of the income from tickets on prizes and none of the prizes can be money. You must sell tickets and declare the winners only during the event itself. The profits must not be for private gain. You can use simple cloakroom tickets for the draw. You don't need to register the draw with your local authority and the ticket prices can vary depending on the quantity sold.

PRIVATE LOTTERIES

A private lottery is one where the tickets are sold to members of a club, people who work together or to people who all live at the same address. You need to include the following information on the ticket:

- the price;
- name and address of the promoter in charge of the lottery;
- the declaration 'sale of tickets is restricted to…';
- the declaration 'no prize won in this lottery shall be paid or delivered by the promoters to any person other than the person to whom the winning ticket was sold by them'.

Tickets can only be sold to the limited group of people defined on the ticket. If you are running a club lottery all income, after printing costs, must be spent on prizes or be given to the club and used for the club's general purposes. If you are running a lottery for people who work or live together all proceeds, after printing costs, must be spent on prizes. You don't need to register the lottery.

SOCIETIES' LOTTERIES

A society lottery is the type you might consider for more general fundraising. There are strict controls on a society lottery because tickets are more widely available to the general public.

You need to register with your local council if you are to run this sort of lottery. If you expect to raise more than £20,000 with one lottery or more than £250,000 in any one calendar year then you need to register with The Gaming Board for Great Britain (see Further information, page 121).

All tickets must contain the following information:

- the name of your organisation;
- the name and address of the person organising the lottery (the promoter);
- the date of the draw when winners will be announced;
- the price of the ticket;
- the ticket number;
- details of the authority you are registered with;
- the declaration that you are a registered charity, if this is the case.

You can't sell tickets in the street or other public places. And no-one under 16 years of age can buy or sell tickets.

You can't give more than 55 per cent of income from ticket sales away as prizes. And no more than 35 per cent of income can be spent on expenses. No more than a total of 80 per cent of income can be spent on prizes and expenses together.

Trading

Another way to raise money from individuals in the community is by selling them something. If you are only doing this on an 'occasional' basis, then this might be accepted as fundraising by the tax authorities. If, however, you are selling goods and services on a regular basis then this might be considered taxable 'trading'.

You should discuss your trading plans with an accountant and a solicitor before setting anything in place. If you are already selling items, such as tea towels or confectionary, then it is worth asking them if you are complying with the law. You might also find it helpful to consult your LEA, the Inland Revenue and the VAT Office when you are at your planning stage. If you are a charity, then you should contact the Charity Commission for advice too. You might find that your local Business Link can provide helpful advice on marketing and business planning.

To make trading worthwhile you need to deal in large volumes and be prepared to invest for the long term. This means planning over at least five years and working with sales worth hundreds or thousands of pounds, rather than tens of pounds. It is essential to plan carefully and to assess whether or not the effort involved is justified by the anticipated levels of return.

The current VAT threshold is £50,000. There are specific and complex rules affecting both charities and educational supplies. It is worth consulting your local VAT office and an accountant for detailed advice.

Here are some initial questions to consider:

- Are you selling second hand/donated goods so that you can convert their value into cash? (This isn't generally considered to be trading.)
- Does your relationship with the LEA restrict what you can do in terms of trading?
- Are you legally able to trade (if you are a charity, does your constitution allow you to do so?). If you are in doubt, consult the Charity Commission.
- Should you set up a subsidiary trading company? (This helps to set the boundaries between your main organisation and the trading company. Debts and liabilities incurred by one will not necessarily affect the other.)
- Are you selling goods which could take trade away from local shops – such goods could include refreshments, merchandise, holidays? (This is considered to be trading.)

- If you have set up a trading subsidiary should it be registered for VAT? Are you over the income threshold, in which case you have to register? Do you want to register voluntarily so that you can claim back VAT on the goods and services you buy?
- If you are registered for VAT are you selling zero-rated goods (which don't have VAT added to them) such as children's clothes and shoes or books? Are you selling goods which should have VAT added? Do you have the systems in place to administer payment of and claims for VAT?

If you set up a separate trading company then this must be shown to cover its own costs – of staffing, premises, equipment, etc. And the charges it makes must be realistic; it mustn't trade at a loss.

Trading can be a highly complicated exercise and must be seen to be worth the investment of time and effort as against some other fundraising activity. In the end it can be simpler to offer goods and services on a non-profit-making basis simply for convenience and promotional purposes, rather than for fundraising.

Personal sponsorships

Sponsored swims, runs, spell-ins and other activities remain popular with many educational fundraisers.

If you are considering a sponsored activity which involves physical effort then you should think through the health and safety issues very carefully. If you are asking young people to participate then you need to consider their personal expectations and abilities and the effect on their self-esteem.

Anyone who has co-ordinated a sponsored activity will be aware of the three phases involved: the nightmare of setting it up; the event itself; and the nightmare of gathering in the money afterwards. It is essential to have clear instructions for all involved and accurate records of everyone's commitments and achievements, along with a strict deadline. The individual competitor must be responsible for collecting all pledges.

On every sponsorship form you need to include:

- the name of the benefiting charity or community group;
- the name and nature of the event;
- where and when the event will take place;
- who is organising the event, with contact details;
- the name of the competitor;
- a statement saying the competitor is responsible for paying over the total amount collected;
- space for a stamp or signature to show what the competitor has achieved.

Careful records are essential for sponsored events and activities. And they play a wider role in fundraising. We turn to this in the next chapter.

CHAPTER 9

Databases

Throughout this guide we have referred to the need to gather and store information about existing and potential supporters. This process might begin when you do an audit of supporters, but it will be an ongoing activity.

In this section we expand on the need to keep track of contacts. Then we talk about some of the legal issues to consider. We go on to describe some of the basic databases you might put in place. And finally we refer to some of the tailor-made fundraising databases.

For more detailed information on this area you might like to refer to the CAF How To... guide *Building a Fundraising Database using your PC* by Peter Flory.

The need to keep track

We have already seen that, together with your colleagues, you have a wide network of contacts. Information about this network needs to be documented in some way if it is to be useful for fundraising. Some of the details may be incomplete and require further research. You can only really see the gaps clearly if you put the information into some kind of database or record.

RECORDING CONTACTS

As you make contact with different people and organisations you will build up a clearer picture of their goals and what they have to offer. This information should be recorded because it is impossible to remember every minor detail. Also it means the information is available for your colleagues to refer or add to.

Making records in this way also helps to avoid embarrassment. You won't ask people for inappropriate support. And you won't go back to the same people too often.

BUILDING UP A PICTURE

You can make a note of people's reactions to your ideas. So, even if they turn down your request for funding, you learn something about what sort of thing they prefer to support.

KEEPING PEOPLE INFORMED

A database can be used as a mailing list for newsletters and promotional literature about projects. This means that you are keeping people informed about your work. You don't even have to send everyone on your database every letter or publication. You can code your records and simply find the appropriate ones to mail out to. It saves you having to sift through your labels by hand.

UPDATING YOUR INFORMATION

A database is only useful, though, if the information is up to date and accurate. If you do a regular mailing then people might tell you if their details have changed. However, you usually need to take a more proactive approach – either ringing round or sending out a print-out of their details to ensure they are correct.

The Data Protection Act

If you have a fundraising database then you have 'computerised information on living, identifiable individuals' and you must register with the Data Protection Registrar. If you should register but don't, then you have committed a criminal offence.

The information you hold might simply be a list of names and addresses. This still qualifies for registration.

There are some exemptions but they aren't likely to be applicable if you are using your database for fundraising purposes. If you want clarification you should ring the Data Protection Registrar Information Line (see Further information, page 127).

To register you should ring a different number, also given in Further information. You usually register for three years and there is a standard fee. When you register you need to give the following information:

- contact details for your organisation;
- a description of the people on your database;
- an outline of the information you hold (or will hold);
- the purposes for which this information will be used;
- how you will obtain this information;
- any people or organisations you might disclose this information to.

There is a specially designed form for charitable organisations with relevant information. But there are no reduced fees or exemptions for fundraising organisations.

There are eight principles with which all registered data users must comply. These are that personal data must be:

- obtained and processed fairly and lawfully;
- held for the lawful purposes described in the data user's register entry;
- used for those purposes, and disclosed only to those people, described in the register entry;
- adequate, relevant and not excessive in relation to the purposes for which they are held;
- accurate and where necessary, kept up to date;
- held no longer than is necessary for the registered purposes;
- accessible to the individual concerned who, where appropriate, has the right to have their information corrected or erased
- surrounded by proper security.

Many of these points encourage good practice in people managing databases. It's worth knowing, though, that if the Data

Protection Registrar thinks you are in breach of one or more of these principles they can take legal action against you.

Paper-based records are currently being brought within the scope of this legislation.

Basic databases

There are a number of standard database packages available which might be adequate for your fundraising records. Some could be included with the 'bundle' of software you get when you buy your computer. Others are available as programmes which can be bought and installed separately.

You have a certain degree of flexibility with packages, such as Microsoft Access and Filemaker Pro. You decide which 'fields' to include (to hold specific bits of information) and how many fields to include per entry or 'record'.

This means that before you set the database up you need to be clear about how it will be used, and what information will be stored.

A TYPICAL SKELETON DATABASE

Here are some of the fields you might want to include in your database:

Contact details:
- name;
- job title (if appropriate);
- organisation (if appropriate);
- address;
- telephone number;
- fax number;
- e-mail.

General:
- last updated;
- type: individual/company/trust/public etc;

- contact within our organisation;
- newsletter recipient: yes/no.

Funding information:
- current funder: yes/no;
- past funder: yes/no;
- past contact;
- funding criteria (if appropriate).

Other:
- support in kind;
- talents/skills.

You might start with this sort of skeleton and then add new fields as your needs change. You might, for instance, hold an event for all friends and supporters. You could add a field to say that they have been invited and another to say whether or not they are able to attend.

If you add a lot of new fields then this can involve quite a bit of work updating and expanding all the information already stored.

Purpose-built fundraising databases

If you want a more powerful system which will allow you to build up mini profiles of your donors then you might consider using a special 'contact management system'. You can use such packages to discover trends, or analyse the make-up of your donor database and any links between funders.

The popular packages include 'The Raiser's Edge', 'Alms', 'Donorflex' and 'Fundmaster'. They offer slightly different functions (reports, mail-merging, automatic form production, sales of merchandise, etc). So, before you look at what is available you should know what you want to achieve.

Donor database software isn't cheap. And you might need to upgrade your computer hardware to run it. Typically, prices range from £500 to £6,000 for a system which will be run on one computer. If you want to set up a database which runs simultaneously on different computers you might have to pay anything between £2,500 and £30,000.

Before buying, you should see the software in action and speak to organisations which are already using it. And you should assess whether the investment is worth it for the scale of fundraising you're involved in.

CHAPTER 10

Building on success

Fundraising is an ongoing process. Every contact you make and every success you have is part of your organisation's and your own personal development. The opportunity is there continually to learn something about other people and about your own strengths and weaknesses. In this section we look at the need to evaluate, celebrate and say 'thank you'.

Evaluation at every stage

Evaluation can take place on a number of levels. It should certainly be a thread that runs through all of your fundraising activity for a number of reasons.

WHY EVALUATE?

Things change:

- times change: new approaches are needed;
- people change: different people have different strengths to offer your fundraising activities;
- needs change: you need to keep your fundraising focused on meeting needs;
- funding opportunities change: new funds are set up, criteria and priorities alter, new companies set up locally.

You learn as you go:

- if something is successful you will want to repeat this, so you should document good practice;
- if something goes wrong, then you will want to make a note of how it could be done differently in future.

Funders want to keep track:

- funders are keen to see that their money is invested effectively;
- many funders set up an independent evaluation process to monitor progress.

EVALUATION ON DIFFERENT LEVELS

Here are some of the different aspects of your fundraising which might require evaluation and review. They include the following elements.

Your fundraising team

Have you got the right mix of people and are they in appropriate roles? Do you need an injection of new ideas and ways of working? Do some people deserve a break?

Your fundraising strategy

Should you be looking at different sources of funding? Have your priorities changed? Has the fundraising climate changed, and do you need to adapt accordingly?

Individual projects

How successfully have you met the perceived need? Was the funding sufficient? Did you allow yourselves enough time to raise the money and do the work? What impact has the project made?

Relationships with different types of funders

Are your approaches to local companies more effective than requests to major trusts? Are parents more comfortable with funding from local government than from businesses? Have you exhausted funds from one particular sector?

Relationships with individual funders

Have you developed partnerships with the local authority? Can your sponsors offer you skills and help in kind? Should any funders be on your committee?

As a result of your evaluation you might feel reassured that you are progressing fairly well. Or you might spot one or two things which could make your fundraising more successful.

Publicising success

When your fundraising is successful, then you should shout about it.

Publicity is an important tool for any fundraiser. The more people who know about your achievements the better.

It all helps to build up your credibility and goodwill in the local community. A pack of press cuttings is an impressive read for any potential sponsor. And the coverage is like a pat on the back to everyone involved, motivating them for future fundraising.

NEWS RELEASES

There are various times when you might have something newsworthy for the media to cover.

Here are some ideas.

Launch announcement

You might launch an appeal or initiative. In your news release you should outline your ideas, explaining the difference that your project could make.

You should be enthusiastic and positive about what you are trying to achieve. Then you can say that you are currently looking for sponsors, for example, to help you carry out your plans.

Well on the way towards target

If you are running an appeal, or if your project needs substantial funding from a variety of sources, then you could issue a news release when you are over half way. This in part acknowledges, and thanks for, the funding you have already received. And it encourages others to give. It keeps you in the public's mind.

Funding received

If you receive a grant to allow your project to go ahead, or if you reach your general target, this is worth shouting about.

Your news release would outline the sums of money received and what you can now achieve.

Project milestones

Throughout the project you will have various news opportunities.

Within any news releases about success, events, etc you should mention the sum of money involved and where the funding came from. It will help those who provided the money to feel appreciated.

Saying thank you

It is important to show your gratitude as you build an ongoing relationship with your funders. Don't just thank people, tell them the difference that their generous support has made.

MEDIA COVERAGE

We have already seen that you can say 'thank you' to fundraisers and funders through good media coverage.

VERBAL AND WRITTEN THANKS

You can say 'thank you' in person and in writing, but it makes more of an impact if you express your gratitude in other ways.

THANK YOU EVENTS

You might organise a 'thank you' event for your funders. This could be an official launch of the project in a high profile location, or it could be a small celebration on your premises. This is a great way to build relationships with supporters, establish personal contact, show them around specific projects they helped to fund, and so on.

CASE STUDY

A group of parents campaigned and fundraised to set up a nursery linked with a primary school. Eventually they raised sufficient money to buy and kit out two mobile rooms, and to staff the nursery. They invited all funders to the opening ceremony. And 'all funders' meant absolutely everyone who had contributed – from a single pen through to hundreds of pounds. The classroom walls were covered with a 'roll of honour' on flipchart sheets. This attached a value to every donation in kind, along with actual cash sums.

LITERATURE

Another way of saying thank you to funders is by mentioning their support in your literature (and making sure they get sent a copy!) This could be in your newsletters and annual report.

Don't let go

A funder isn't just for Christmas, a funder is for life. Once someone has provided you with some support you should follow this up, keep in touch and try to develop an ongoing relationship with them. You should never harass them in any way, but try to keep lines of communication open even if it's one way, with you sending the occasional newsletter.

Further information and advice

Throughout this guide we have mentioned a number of organisations and initiatives. In this section we provide contact details.

STATUTORY CONTACTS

Charity Commission
Harmsworth House
13–15 Bouverie Street
London EC4Y 8DP
Tel 0870-333 0123

Gaming Board for Great Britain
Berkshire House
168–173 High Holborn
London WC1V 7AA
Tel 0171-306 6200

Health Education Authority
Trevalyan House
30 Great Peter Street
London SW1P 2HW
Tel 0171-222 5300

National Consumer Council
20 Grosvenor Gardens
London SW1W 0DH
Tel 0171-730 3469

National Association of Councils of Voluntary Service (NACVS)
Third Floor, Arundel Court
177 Arundel Street
Sheffield S1 2NV
Tel 0114-278 6636

Performing Rights Society
29–33 Berners Street
London W1P 4AA
Tel 0171-306 4233

Publications

The Councils' Handbook (details of all local authorities in the UK) published by CD.C Publishing Ltd, 7 Marsham Street, London SW1P 3DW
Tel 0171–222 2772
Fax 0171–222 2773

TRUSTS AND FOUNDATIONS

Association of Charitable Foundations
4 Bloomsbury Square
London
WC1A 2RL
Tel 0171–404 1338
Fax 0171–831 3881

Association of Community Trusts and Foundations (ACTAF)
4 Bloomsbury Square
London WC1A 2RL
Tel 0171-831 0033

Foundation for Sport and the Arts
PO Box 20
Liverpool
L13 1HB
Tel 0151–259 5505
Fax 0151–230 0664

National Endowment for Science, Technology and the Arts (NESTA)
2–4 Cockspur Street
London
SW1Y 5DH
Tel 0171–211 2850
Fax 0171–211 2875

LOTTERY CONTACT NUMBERS

Arts Council of England
Tel 0171-312 0123

Arts Council of Northern Ireland
Tel 01232-667 000

Arts Council of Wales
Tel 01222-376 500

Scottish Arts Council
Tel 0131-226 6051

English Sports Council
Tel 0345-649 649

Scottish Sports Council
Tel 0131-339 9000

Sports Council for Northern Ireland
Tel 01232-382 222

Sports Council for Wales
Tel 01222-300 500

Heritage Lottery Fund
Tel 0171-591 6041

National Lottery Charities Board
Tel 0345-919191

Millennium Commission
Tel 0171-880 2030

New Opportunities Fund
Tel 0171-222 3084

COMPANY FUNDRAISING

Business in the Community
44 Baker Street
London W1M 1DM
Tel 0171-224 1600

Confederation of British Industry (CBI)
103 New Oxford Street
London
WC1A 1DU
Tel 0171-379 7400
Fax 0171-240 0988

TEC National Council
Westminster Tower
3 Albert Embankment
London SE1 7SX
Tel 0171-735 0010

Publications

The *Directory of Educational Contacts* lists organisations linking business and education to raise standards in schools and colleges. It is published free by **Business in the Community** and more information is available from the education information officer. *Tel* 0171-224 1600.

The *Directory of Teaching Materials* from Business for Schools and Colleges is published free by the University of Warwick's **Centre for Education and Industry** (CEI), University of Warwick, Coventry CV4 7AL.

CHARITIES AND COMMUNITY ORGANISATIONS

Community Education Development Centre
Woodway Park School
Wigston Road
Coventry
CV2 2RH
Tel 01203-655 700
Fax 01203-655 701

The Community Education Development Centre is a national organisation for community-based learning. It aims to promote a fairer distribution of learning opportunities, particularly to individuals and groups who have previously benefited least from education. It runs innovative partnership projects which focus on areas such as health, social change, family learning and personal development. It has a pilot project in which schools are acting as community regenerators and playing an active role in local economic development. It has also established many neighbourhood groups for local economic development.

The CEDC publishes a range of books on inclusive education, model development projects and community partnerships.

Crime Concern
Beaver House
147–150 Victoria Road
Swindon
SN1 3BU
Tel 01793-863 500
Fax 01793-514 654

Crime Concern runs a number of youth action partnership projects with schools throughout England and Wales. The organisation has also set up a number of family literacy projects to encourage pre-school and primary school children from disadvantaged neighbourhoods.

Include
8 High Street
Ely
CB7 4JY
Tel 01353-650 303
Fax 01353-650 304

Include runs projects which aim to reintegrate young people into mainstream education, training and employment through innovative, multi-agency working; offering a long-term strategy for tackling the crisis of social exclusion.

Industry in Education (IIE)
Victoria Chambers
Victoria Road
Harpenden
AL5 4EA
Tel 01582-760 078
Fax 01582-760 166

Industry in Education aims to improve mutual understanding between education and industry. It has produced a number of interesting reports, including 'Building a Stronger Partnership Between Business and Education'.

Kids' Club Network
Bellerive House
3 Muirfield Crescent
London
E14 9SZ
Tel 0171-512 2112
Fax 0171-512 2010

Kids' Club Network provides advice, publications and support to people setting up childcare projects for school age children. It publishes a fundraising guide with advice on securing money for luxuries and funds to stay afloat (price £6).

FUNDRAISING DIRECTORIES AND GUIDES

A Guide to Fundraising for School Grounds
published by **Learning Through Landscapes** (in association with the Directory of Social Change). Contact Learning Through Landscapes, Third Floor, Southside Offices, The Law Courts, Winchester, S023 9DL. *Tel* 01962-846 258. Price £8.95

The Directory of Grant Making Trusts
published by the **Charities Aid Foundation**, Kings Hill, West Malling, Kent ME19 4TA (see other publications from CAF).

The Education Funding Guide and School Fundraising
published by **The Directory of Social Change**, 24 Stephenson Way, London NW1 2DP. *Tel* 0171-209 5151. Price £15.95

PROFESSIONAL FUNDRAISERS

Institute of Charity Fundraising Managers (ICFM)
1 Nine Elms Lane
London
SW8 5NQ
Tel 0171-627 3436
Fax 0171-627 3508

Publications

Legacy Fundraising
published jointly by CAF and ICFM, editor Sebastian Wilberforce. Contact the **Charities Aid Foundation.** *Tel* 01732-520 000. Price £14.95

DATA PROTECTION

The Office of The Data Protection Registrar
Wycliffe House
Water Lane
Wilmslow
CK9 5AF
Tel 01625-545 700
Information line 01625-545 745
Registration line 01625-545 740

PARENT-TEACHER ASSOCIATIONS

National Confederation of Parent-Teacher Associations
2 Ebbsfleet Estate
Stonebridge Road
Gravesend
Kent
DA11 9DZ
Tel 01474-560 618
Fax 01474-564 418

INFORMATION ON EUROPEAN FUNDING

Information on European funding is avalable from your TEC or LEC or from the following Website
http://europa.eu.int/en/comm/dg22/socrates.html

FUNDRAISING SOFTWARE

More information on FunderFinder software, designed to help you work your way through a trust directory, can be obtained by contacting **FunderFinder**. *Tel* 0113-243 3008.

About CAF

CAF, Charities Aid Foundation, is a registered charity with a unique mission – to increase the substance of charity in the UK and overseas. It provides services that are both charitable and financial which help donors make the most of their giving and charities make the most of their resources.

Many of CAF's publications reflect the organisation's purpose: *Dimensions of the Voluntary Sector* offers the definitive financial overview of the UK voluntary sector, while the *Directory of Grant Making Trusts* provides the most comprehensive source of funding information available.

As an integral part of its activities, CAF works to raise standards of management in voluntary organisations. This includes the making of grants by its own Grants Council, sponsorship of the Charity Annual Report and Accounts Awards, seminars, training courses and the Charities Annual Conference, the largest regular gathering of key people from within the voluntary sector. In addition, Charitynet (www.charitynet.org) is now established as the leading Internet site on voluntary action.

For decades, CAF has led the way in developing tax-effective services to donors, and these are now used by more than 250,000 individuals and 2,000 of the UK's leading companies, between them giving £150 million each year to charity. Many are also using CAF's CharityCard, the world's first debit card designed exclusively for charitable giving. CAF's unique range of investment and administration services for charities includes the CafCash High Interest Cheque Account, two common investment funds for longer-term investment and a full appeals and subscription management service.

CAF's activities are not limited to the UK, however. Increasingly, CAF is looking to apply the same principles and develop similar services internationally, in its drive to increase the substance of charity across the world. CAF has offices and sister organisations in the United States, Bulgaria, South Africa, Russia, India and Brussels.

For more information about CAF, please visit www.charitynet.org/caf

Other publications from CAF

How To series

A series of one-stop guides on a variety of core activities, the titles appearing in the CAF 'How To' series are designed to provide both volunteers supporting smaller charities - in either an official or an unofficial capacity - and inexperienced salaried staff with practical information and guidance on good practice.

THE TREASURER'S HANDBOOK *Ian Caulfeild Grant*

ISBN 1-85934-018-0 £7.95

Published August 1996

Recent legislation has reinforced the crucial role of the treasurer in voluntary organisations of all sizes, whilst the introduction of the SORP is intended to lead to a greater uniformity of practice throughout the sector.

As a treasurer's duties become more onerous, their personal, legal liability for the 'prudent management' of their organisation is thrown sharply into relief. Yet many volunteer treasurers do not have even a basic understanding of book-keeping activities.

In straightforward language, avoiding financial jargon, *The Treasurer's Handbook* outlines a treasurer's key tasks, proposes appropriate procedures and explains the basics of financial management.

APPLYING TO A GRANT MAKING TRUST A guide for fundraisers *Anne Villemur*

ISBN 1-85934-033-4 £7.95

Published February 1997

Grant making trusts of all sizes complain that many of the funding applications that they receive fail either to match their stated funding priorities or to provide a coherent explanation of the project or programme for which support is being sought. Consequently, they are not eligible for consideration.

In response to this situation, and drawing on the author's years of experience as editor of *The Directory of Grant Making Trusts*, this book provides step by step guidance in drawing up a well-rounded 'case for support' which contains all the information that trustees require when considering an application.

BUILDING A FUNDRAISING DATABASE USING YOUR PC

Peter Flory

ISBN 1-85934-104-7 £11.95

Published June 1999

ORGANISING A MILLENIUM EVENT *Karen Gilchrist*

ISBN 1-85934-104-7 £9.95

Published June 1999

Other publications

THE DIRECTORY OF GRANT MAKING TRUSTS 1999–2000 16TH EDITION

ISBN 1-85934-078-4 £89.95 (3 volumes)

Published January 1999

The *Directory of Grant Making Trusts (DGMT)* keeps fundraisers in touch with changes in trusts' funding priorities. Its extensive indexing allows great precision in the targeting of trusts – thus reducing the flow of irrelevant applications and saving time and money at both ends.

The information published in the *DGMT* is the result of extensive research and close liaison with the trust community; it provides the most comprehensive picture of UK trusts currently published. As well as listing over 3,500 trusts – of which 1,500 are new to this edition – the Directory now features top 10 sample grants for hundreds of trusts and a new index by grant type. With the addition of the new third volume providing detailed commentaries on 250 of the major trusts, the *DGMT* now truly represents a complete, one-stop information shop for the trust fundraiser.

And it works! Feedback from the fundraising community has been overwhelmingly positive. An essential tool for every trust fundraiser, in most cases it more than pays for itself – it does so many, many times over.

Focus series

SCHOOLS, COLLEGES AND EDUCATIONAL ESTABLISHMENTS

ISBN 1-85934-053-9 £19.95

Designed to make the search for funds easier still, many directories from the *Focus Series* will collect together, in individual volumes, details of trusts which have expressed an intention to support charitable activity in particular fields. These directories focus on trusts supporting causes associated with particular projects. In addition to comprehensive details of the future funding priorities of the trusts listed, information is also provided on recent grants they have made.

These directories will give grant-seekers working in the relevant fields a head-start in identifying sympathetic trusts and presenting well-tailored funding applications.

Index